COMMITTED TO CHRIST

Adult Readings and Study Book

COMMITTED TO CHRIST:
Six Steps to a Generous Life

Program Guide With CD-ROM

Lays out the basic plans for the campaign, including schedules, team roles, sermon illustrations, worship helps, letters, and commitment cards. Art, files, schedules, and task lists are found on the accompanying CD-ROM. 978-1-4267-4351-1

Adult Readings and Study Book

Designed for use in the six-week small group study that undergirds the program, as well as by others participating in the program. 978-1-4267-4352-8

Small Group Leader Guide

Contains everything a leader needs to organize and run a small group or Sunday school class in support of the program, including discussion questions, activities, and flexible session lengths and formats. 978-1-4267-4353-5

Devotional Book: 40 Devotions for a Generous Life

Devotional companion for program participants. Each of the forty devotions includes Scripture, a brief story or meditation, and a prayer. 978-1-4267-5488-3

DVD: Worship Videos

Designed for the worship experience, this DVD contains seven pre-worship gathering time loops and seven lead-ins. 978-1-4267-4355-9

CD-ROM: Tweets, Posts, and Prayers

Contains devotions and prayers for use during the program to build interest and excitement using social media: texts, Twitter, blogs, and email. 843504026912

Preview Book: Six Steps to a Generous Life

A pocket-sized book designed to introduce the congregation to the themes of the six-week Committed to Christ experience. 978-1-4267-4690-1

Committed to Christ Kit

One of each component. 843504028886

BOB CROSSMAN

COMMITTED
TO CHRIST

Six Steps to a Generous Life

Adult Readings and Study Book

ABINGDON PRESS
Nashville

Committed to Christ
Adult Readings and Study Book

Bob Crossman

Library of Congress Cataloging-in-Publication applied for.

ISBN 978-1-4267-4352-8

12 13 14 15 16 17 18 19 20 21 — 10 9 8 7 6 5 4 3 2 1

MANUFACTURED IN THE UNITED STATES OF AMERICA

CONTENTS

INTRODUCTION

When I was about seven years old, my family and I went to a weekend retreat at the United Methodist Lakeview Christian Retreat Center in Palestine, Texas, a beautiful 1300-acre camp north of Houston. One afternoon, when my mother and father were at a parents' group and I was supposed to be with the children's group, I decided to skip the planned activity and go for a private walk instead.

At this retreat center there was a small lake near the main building. By Arkansas standards, it was really a pond, about 1000 feet across. A determined seven-year-old, I decided I was going to walk around the lake. I followed along the shoreline and everything was going fine until I reached the far side, where a creek fed into the lake. I was still determined to complete the circuit, but my path was blocked by soft, muddy ground, cattails, and brush. The wet ground forced me to leave the lakeshore and follow the creek bed until I could find a narrow spot where I could step over without getting muddy.

The forest along the creek quickly overtook me. The dense woods, underbrush, thistles, and thorns were so thick that I lost sight of the lake and the little creek. Well, as you might have guessed, I was lost.

It was an hour, maybe two, before I found my way back. I followed the creek to the lake, where I eventually returned to the retreat center and my anxious parents. It had been a pretty scary afternoon for a seven-year-old.

A few years later, when I was in the Boy Scouts, I paid close attention to the scoutmaster's lessons on map reading and use of a compass. After the training, with compass in hand, we could find any location he marked on the map.

Today, there is a new system that helps us find our destination. Twenty-four global positioning satellites orbit the earth. With an inexpensive GPS device, it is now possible to discover your exact location on the planet. With such a GPS device, a hunter, a soldier, or a cruise missile can arrive within fifty inches of any spot on earth. Today, my car even has a GPS device. Beginning at any point in North America, I can type in an address or push the "home" button, and the GPS voice gives me directions to my desired destination.

Have you ever been lost? There are lots of ways it can happen: walking around a lake, turning down a wrong street, or wandering around the supermarket, trying to find paper towels.

There are other ways we can get lost that have far greater implications. We can be lost in our vocation, our marriage, our spiritual life, or our direction as a church.

In all these situations, we tend to lose our focus: we forget what is important, or become distracted and wander off course. As a pastor, I've watched some of my members lose their way at the office or in the home, when they forget about core values such as honesty and integrity.

Committed to Christ: Six Steps to a Generous Life will offer a road map, a series of paths, a journey toward holy living and mature Christian discipleship. It offers a vision—what I hope and believe is a clear 20/20 vision—of six expectations the Lord has of those who seek to call themselves disciples. Such a vision can have powerful implications.

I discovered the power of vision in my own life. When I was in the fifth grade, my father invited me to write down what I wanted to be when I grew up. It was a simple childhood exercise and was quickly forgotten. Shortly before my father's death, he showed me a scrap of paper he had carried in his billfold for forty years. Though it was faint,

I could still clearly read my own childhood printing: "To be a preacher, and to have a PhD in theology." I was amazed to see the written evidence of my childhood hope, and to realize that it had been fulfilled by my Doctor of Ministry degree, ordination, and thirty years of pastoral service.

I've also discovered the power of vision for a local church. When I was a young pastor, I invited the leadership of my new church to meet in my dining room every Wednesday evening our first summer on staff together. We met to pray and work as we discerned a vision for our church and set benchmarks for several areas of ministry. One benchmark set by the leadership included: In six years our worship attendance will grow from 45 to 450. Six years later, that congregation averaged 444, and two years later it grew to 503. Another benchmark set by the leadership: In six years we will have a building that meets our needs. Six years later, that congregation had a new million-dollar building. A third benchmark: Within six years, six people in our congregation will experience a call to full-time Christian ministry. Six years later, six members of that congregation were seminary students, and today all six are in ministry.

Great things can happen when a congregation, or an individual, has a sense of God's direction, purpose, and vision.

Committed to Christ: Six Steps to a Generous Life invites you to have a vision, perhaps a clear 20/20 vision, of Christian discipleship. You will be invited to grow, step by step, in your relationship with Jesus Christ, through prayer, Bible reading, worship attendance, witness, financial gifts, and service; and, you will be asked to fill out a commitment card each week to help you plan that growth.

Are you ready to take the first steps this year? Do you have a clear vision of what the Lord expects of faithful followers?

CHEESY GIVING?

Ed Stetzer

Throughout life we are presented with opportunities to exercise good stewardship related to finances. Sometimes we make good decisions and sometimes we make bad decisions, but we seek always to honor Christ in the decisions we make. An interaction with one of my children about snack food provided humorous but real insight into this struggle.

Recently, around the time I was teaching on stewardship at our church, I was drawn into an argument with my middle daughter over an empty box of Cheez-Its in our cabinet. Convinced that I had eaten all those tasty little crackers, my daughter became obsessed with getting her own Cheez-Its to replace them. Her actions were like those of a person convinced there were no more Cheez-Its in the world! The truth was, she did not believe that her father could or would give her more of this favorite food.

During the teaching series at our church, we created a big box of Cheez-Its to put onstage to serve as a metaphor. We realized that, for some of us, fear (of not having something) leads to greed (I want that thing) leads to idolatry (I worship that thing) leads to bondage (it rules and imprisons me). My daughter's reaction to the empty box is an example of our own lack of faith that our Father can provide for our needs. It also illustrates how anything can derail our willingness to honor God by being good financial stewards.

Ed Stetzer is President of LifeWay Research, one of the best and most-quoted Christian research organizations in the world. He has planted churches in multiple states, trained pastors across the U.S. and on six continents, and taught at fourteen seminaries. Author or co-author of twelve books, Stetzer is a leading voice among evangelicals. He is a contributing editor or columnist for several publications, including Christianity Today, Outreach Magazine, The Christian Post, *and* Facts and Trends.

AN INVITATION
TO FOLLOW CHRIST

A few years ago I visited Joplin United Methodist Church, west of Hot Springs, Arkansas. They are a fairly new congregation, having moved into their first building about fifteen years ago. I noticed next to the front door a doghouse that had a small cross on top. Inside, a dog lay on a bed of fresh straw and a soft towel.

I asked the pastor, Rev. David Jones, about the dog. He said, "That is our church dog, and notice that we have a second doghouse nearby for guests that drop by to visit." The church dog walked over to greet me—here was a mixed breed with only three legs, welcoming visitors.

What a powerful testimony and witness! The church dog, without saying a word, proclaimed that if you have been wounded by life, if you have been hurt, if you have been beaten or crushed, if you are limping like a three-legged dog—whatever condition you find yourself in, you are welcome to the house of the Lord.

I have an invitation for you. Whether you are wounded or standing tall, I invite you to begin a journey. This journey has been described in many ways: making a spiritual quest, growing up in Christ, proclaiming your relationship with God, putting on the whole armor of

God. However you choose to describe it, the journey begins today and continues until the end of time.

This journey is not a solo trip; we are traveling together in relationship with other Christians. The journey has many steps; some of the most important involve prayer, Bible reading, worship, witness, financial giving, and service. All of us—those who are strong and those who feel wounded—are invited to stand close to one another, lean on each other, and learn from each other as we journey together toward a deeply devoted relationship with Christ.

*   *   *

Many of you grew up in a church where Christianity was just a tradition. You were baptized because it was expected of you. You joined the church because you were supposed to. You attended worship and went through the motions, but doing so did not change your life. Perhaps you thought, "This is what Christianity means. This is what Christians do."[1]

For some of you, there has been a change. At some point you discovered that Christianity isn't simply an intellectual decision to "believe in God." It is the most profound, dynamic, exciting, passionate, and joy-filled life that anyone can live. In that season of discovery, you began a journey with Christ. You began to grow toward being a fully devoted disciple of Jesus Christ.

In John 10:10, we find Jesus saying, "I am come that you might have life, and that you might have it more abundantly" (KJV). The primary mission of a healthy church is to help everyone discover the "abundant" life in Jesus Christ by becoming a fully devoted disciple: to surrender completely to God; to serve God and be like Jesus; to love the Lord your God with all your heart, mind, soul, and strength; and to love your neighbor as you love yourself.

For each of us, that goal can be described in even simpler terms: to be a faithful disciple with head, heart, and hands.

John Wesley, Anglican priest and founder of the eighteenth-century Methodist movement, was a preacher's kid. From Wesley's perspective at his father's side, he saw lots of churchgoers who lived without purpose, claiming to be Christians because they went to church and had been baptized. Wesley believed there must be more to Christianity than sitting in worship on Sunday morning and going through a baptism ceremony.[2] He began to seek the answer to some basic questions:

> *What does it mean to be a disciple of Jesus Christ?*
> *What does the Lord expect of his faithful followers?*
> *What "holy habits" should be present in the believer's life?*

After years of thought and practice, Wesley eventually made a distinction between what he called the "almost Christian" and the "altogether Christian." The almost Christian, Wesley preached in a famous sermon, will attend worship every Sunday; pray; respect common honesty; never steal a neighbor's property; feed the hungry; refrain from cursing or gossiping; and may use time and talents to serve God. Wesley, describing himself in his early years, said,

> It is possible to go this far and yet be but almost a Christian. I used all diligence to avoid evil and keep a clear conscience. I was careful of my time, using every opportunity to do good. I was constantly using all the means of grace. With God as my witness, I did this with all sincerity, having a real desire to serve God. Yet, all that time I was only almost a Christian.[3]

Wesley declared that the "altogether Christian," by contrast, has several additional characteristics. The altogether Christian has a heart filled with love of God and neighbor; believes the historical doctrines of the church are true; believes the Holy Scriptures are true; and above all has faith in the saving power of Jesus Christ.[4]

✳   ✳   ✳

Growing up, I learned about Christ through my parents' words and actions. I clearly remember a family trip in Colorado to see the Royal Gorge near Canyon City. It was an amazing sight. The Arkansas River flowed through the bottom of the canyon, while a thousand feet above, a twelve-hundred-foot bridge stretched across a canyon. Although the bridge was built over eighty years ago, it is still the highest bridge in

North America and today remains one of Colorado's most-visited tourist sites.

As our family stood on the edge of that great canyon, admiring the span of the bridge, my father made it a teachable moment by saying, "I'm reminded of something when I look at this bridge. I am reminded that Jesus offers to be your bridge and mine. Jesus offers to carry us to heaven, where we can never go on our own."

Because of my parents' faithful worship attendance, I have many memories of Sunday school, youth hayrides, church-sponsored camping trips, confirmation classes, and chances to serve as an acolyte and light the candles at the beginning of worship.

I also remember the weekend when my relationship with the church changed. It happened one Sunday morning when a student from the campus ministry at Hendrix College spoke briefly in worship. There was something in her words that impressed me. She spoke of Jesus Christ as if she knew him personally. She spoke of prayer as if God actually listened. She spoke of Christianity as if it had offered her a sense of purpose and direction to her daily life. Hearing her, I knew she had a relationship with Jesus Christ that I deeply needed too.

The next Sunday, in response to the closing invitation, I remember praying,

> God I do believe in you. I believe you created this world and created me too. I believe in your son Jesus. I believe Jesus died on the cross to forgive my sins. Dear God, forgive me for all the times I have messed up. Help me, God, to be the kind of person you might be proud of.

It wasn't a fancy prayer, but it was the most genuine prayer I had prayed in my life. That week, at the age of seventeen, I felt a desire to grow as a Christian. I began to read the New Testament and pray. With the permission of our youth minister, I led a Friday night youth discussion group. With God's help, I started to change my life.

Now, I don't think I had been going straight to hell on Saturday, and suddenly on Sunday I was headed to heaven. But I do know that on that particular Sunday, I made a decision to follow Jesus Christ.

In the days after that decision, I began to feel uncomfortable with my language. I had developed a bad habit of telling jokes that I wouldn't tell my Sunday school teacher, pastor, or mother. I decided that they were not the kind of jokes I should be telling anyone now that I had invited Jesus to "walk beside me." It was a hard habit to break. To help me remember my decision, I started carrying my wallet in a different pocket, wearing my watch on a different wrist, and wearing a cross under my shirt. I also made a covenant with my best friend, and together we helped each other stop this bad habit.

Six months later, when I had made great progress with my language, the Lord wasn't finished with me. Step-by-step, month-by-month, it was as if the Lord placed another invitation in front of me. I felt that I was on a journey through the woods, late at night in the darkness. I could not see where the path ended, but I could see three or four feet ahead. When I took a step, then I could see one step farther as I began to follow Jesus Christ.

I was on a journey, not to earn salvation, but toward holy living in response to the salvation I had received. The Lord continued to invite me to take another step closer and to live more faithfully as one of his disciples.

I wish I could report that I have completed the journey. I have not. I am not perfect. I still sin. I fall short of the goal that Christ has placed in front of me. There have been seasons when I have said, "Lord, just leave me alone. I've grown in the faith all I care to right now." But, thank God, the Lord has not left me alone. As the hymn says, the Lord continued to walk with me and talk with me. The Lord invited me to continue the journey through daily prayer, Bible reading, faithful worship attendance, winsome witness, financial giving that is growing to the Biblical minimum standard of a 10% tithe, and service to others in Jesus' name. It seems that one month I will take three steps forward, then the next month four steps back. And yet, by God's grace, as the months go by I've traveled forward; I've changed; I've been molded by the very Spirit of God.

*   *   *

While attending graduate school, I met a man who taught me that a commitment to Christ is more valuable than silver and gold, and worth more than any earthly kingdom. I was in training to be a pastor at Southern Methodist University. To help cover the expenses of tuition, room, and board, I worked at the school serving as a hall director, shelving books in the library, delivering *The Daily Campus* newspaper, and working as a custodian in one of the residence halls. One of my fellow student janitors was from Nigeria. His name was Lawrence Ladigbolu. Together we mopped hallways, waxed floors, and cleaned the public restrooms.

Lawrence was a tall, handsome man, with initiation scars on each side of his face. The facial scars looked as if a lion's claws had carved deep grooves down each side of his face. Lawrence was also a man of faith. Whenever I asked about his home and family, Lawrence would change the subject. Lawrence would rather talk about Jesus, and his desire to return home as a Methodist preacher.

I was a poor student from Arkansas, and Lawrence was a poor student from Nigeria. However, Lawrence hadn't always been poor.

At birth he was given the name His Royal Highness Prince Ayo Ladigbolu. As the first son of King Ayo Ladigbolu, the prince was heir to the throne of the ancient Yoruba Empire, as well as to property, palaces, and a kingdom of twelve million subjects. Being the first son of the king, the prince was taught by the finest Islamic scholars in Nigeria. He became a leader in the Muslim faith of his country. He admitted that many times he joined in the abuse of Christians, even the stoning of Christians, for following the teachings of Jesus instead of Mohammad.

On October 1, 1962, in a conversation with a Methodist missionary, Prince Ladigbolu accepted Jesus Christ as his Lord and Savior. He later reported, "I asked Jesus Christ to come into my heart, to cleanse it of all sin and to make me a child of God. Right there and then, I felt as if ice-cold water were dripping from heaven through my head and into the rest of my body. It was a most pleasant and refreshing feeling."

Two months later, the king learned that his son had entered a Methodist church. Soon after, the entire family confronted him. Sitting on the throne, his father shouted, "Welcome back from *church*! Why in the world would you enter a *church*?"

For the first time, Lawrence confessed his belief in Jesus Christ to his family. The king demanded that he renounce Jesus Christ. His mother fell to her knees in tears and begged him, "Son, don't you know that I could be killed along with you?" Lawrence replied, "Mother, there is no going back. I have tasted the Lord Jesus Christ and found him sweeter than honey."

Because of his decision to follow Christ instead of Mohammad, Lawrence gave up his kingdom of twelve million subjects. He chose to preach Christ and Christ crucified, sacrificing his inheritance to follow that calling.

In fear of his own life, Lawrence escaped Nigeria with the help of the Methodist Church and traveled to Dallas, Texas, where he enrolled in Southern Methodist University's Perkins School of Theology to study for the ministry. To help pay his tuition, room, and board, the former prince cleaned toilets with a poor boy from Arkansas.

Lawrence Ladigbolu writes, "I lost all my power, prestige, money, and land associated with my earthly royal birthright. I have no regrets today because I have gained a more glorious crown, the crown of life."[5]

*　　*　　*

The conversion experienced by a Nigerian prince can happen for all of us today. By using Committed to Christ: Six Steps to a Generous Life, you and your church can continue your journey with God. You will be invited to become a high-expectation congregation that looks for its people to pray daily, read the Bible regularly, attend worship faithfully, witness willingly, give sacrificially, and serve gladly.

Committed to Christ: Six Steps to a Generous Life does not propose that this is simply a nice idea, but rather that faithful discipleship truly matters to God. It will encourage you to grow, step by step, toward becoming a deeply devoted disciple of Jesus Christ—a journey worth giving one's life to.

Lord, could you love someone like me? Could you accept someone like me? Would you allow someone like me to be your disciple? Lord, you know I am not perfect. You know all the mistakes I've made and pain I've caused through the years. Forgive me. Forgive me for my past. Come into my heart, like you came into Lawrence's heart, to cleanse it of all sin and make me a child of God. Accept me as one of your disciples, and send your Holy Spirit to give me the guidance and strength to faithfully follow you from this day forward. Lord, I do want to begin today a journey toward becoming a deeply devoted disciple of yours. Amen.

ACCEPTING CHRIST AS LORD AND SAVIOR

Scott J. Jones

I was raised in The United Methodist Church, but it was more of a social experience than a true conversion and commitment to Christ. When I left home, I quit worshiping. I didn't attend Sunday school. It wasn't that I was hostile to Christianity; I just thought organized religion wasn't worth the time. I knew that the church did good things but wasn't sure about the existence of God. Most important, I didn't have faith. I wondered what it meant to believe. I found answers through two conversations, one book, and prayer.

The first conversation came when I was hitchhiking. A truck driver picked me up, and for two hours he shared his faith with me. The man's certainty about salvation was attractive. Afterward I thought, "I want what that man has."

A year later, a friend gave me a copy of C. S. Lewis's book, *The Lion, the Witch and the Wardrobe*, the first volume in *The Chronicles of Narnia* trilogy. For the first time I was exposed to powerful images that made sense of basic Christian teachings.

The second conversation was with a college friend who told me about giving her life to Christ and the peace that comes from surrendering one's heart. After that, I began praying that God would zap me with a powerful conversion experience. That experience never came. But a year later, alone in a campus ministry chapel, I was given the sense of peace my friend had described, and I came to know the love of Christ deep in my heart.

I had become a disciple of Jesus.

Scott J. Jones, bishop of the Kansas Area of The United Methodist Church since 2004, served on the faculty of Perkins School of Theology, Southern Methodist University, from 1997 to 2004, where he taught the evangelism history of Christianity and Wesley studies.

1.
LET US PRAY

At the age of eighteen I enrolled in Arkansas Tech University. During my first week on campus, a fellow classmate named Craig invited me to join the college choir. My immediate response was, "Oh no. You don't want me. I've never been in a choir." Craig insisted that I try the choir for just one month and would not let me decline the offer.

Something happened during that first month in the college choir. I discovered that if I stood close to Craig—my friend who could read music, my friend who knew when to start singing and when to stop, my friend who could hit the right note every time, my friend the voice major—if I stood close to Craig, then I could sing too!

Something like that happens in church. We are not all mature, deeply devoted disciples of Jesus Christ. We are not all at the same place in that journey. We are not all at the same level of maturity. Some have an amazing prayer life. Others are well-seasoned volunteers with many blisters they received by serving in Jesus' name. Still others have discovered the joy of tithing and double-tithing their financial resources, generously supporting the Sunday offering in worship. By standing close to each other, we find inspiration, courage, and the guidance we need to begin the journey toward Christian maturity. Many of today's prayer warriors, at some point in life, began when their grandmother said, "Hold your hands like this. Close your eyes. Repeat after me: 'Now I lay me down to sleep. I pray the Lord my soul to keep.' "

This week we begin our journey through Committed to Christ: Six Steps to a Generous Life. In the weeks ahead we will be invited, in a variety of ways, to take one new step in each of six areas of discipleship. We are invited to take these six steps, not to earn our salvation, but rather in response to the salvation we have already received. Today, the invitation is to grow one step in our prayer life.

To grow toward a deeply devoted prayer life, one must pray.

For the past twenty years, I have served as the secretary of the Annual Conference for the United Methodist churches in Arkansas. I have a staff of thirteen who help me during the conference by taking minutes, typing reports, perfecting budgets, insuring that parliamentary procedure is followed, setting up tables and chairs, recording the sessions, and live-streaming on the Internet. At the end of the 20 hours of business meetings, my staff produces a 700-page journal that accurately records all the proceedings and reports from 700 churches. To accomplish this task in three days takes a fair number of computers and electronic equipment.

The technical language used to describe computer capability can be overwhelming. A young sales associate at an electronics store recently said to me, "You've got to see the new computer. I just bought one myself. It's some machine. It has a 2.3 ghz quad-core Intel processor, L3 cache, four gigabites of memory, 8x Super Drive, FaceTime high-definition camera, seventeen-inch display, and stereo speakers with subwoofers. I mean, this is some machine." After this elaborate description I asked, "What are you going to do with that computer?" "Well," he said, "I type my class notes on it."

Today we have more computing power on our PCs than the Apollo astronauts had when they journeyed to the moon and back. And yet, in many homes these amazing tools are used simply to take notes. As followers of Christ, we have an unbelievable resource in prayer: we have the opportunity for a personal relationship with Christ that could transform our lives; we have the opportunity for joy and strength; and we have the invitation to a daily walk with God. And yet, what do we do with this great resource? Far too many of us only send God a short five-second note about once a week. We miss out on all the power of prayer.

During this program, the six steps will help you focus on your spiritual life. The first step is about prayer—how it can transform your life and what it really is all about. It is my hope that as we learn to pray, we can all grow in our own walks with Christ. It is my hope that wherever you are in your prayer life, you will "climb one step" in your life of prayer.

* * *

I've got a story for you that is *not* from the Bible.

Jesus and his twelve disciples were sitting down to eat. Jesus turned to Peter and asked, "Peter, would you say the prayer before we eat?"

Everyone bowed his head and Peter prayed out loud:

O existential manifestation of the cosmic force, the ground of our being, and first principle of essential causality: Hear our supplication, O mighty One of the universe. Pour upon all who are any ways afflicted, or distressed, the continual dew of thy blessing, that it may please thee to comfort and relieve their several necessities, giving them a happy issue out of all their afflictions. And, we beseech thee, give us that due sense of all thy mercies, that our hearts may be unfeignedly thankful. Fulfill now the petitions of thy servants, as may be most expedient for them, for the sake of him who ever-liveth to make intercession for us. Bless O Sovereign these thy gifts before us, that our bodies may be strengthened, in the name of him who made, by his one oblation, a full and sufficient sacrifice. Amen.

Jesus lifted his head, looked at Peter, and asked, "Say what?"

* * *

It's a shame, isn't it, how complicated and difficult we've made prayer. It's gotten lost in all kinds of theological technicalities, liturgical formalities, and religious language. It's no wonder today that so many people don't know how to make heads or tails out of prayer. We are surrounded by people who want to have a wonderful relationship with God. But sometimes when they turn to the church and say, "Teach us to pray," they get a response that does not feed their spiritual hunger at all.

Adam Hamilton put it this way: "God offers us an ocean, and we choose a puddle instead."[6] God invites you and me to go deep. God offers to give us the depth of his presence in our lives, the depth of a life filled with joy, and the depth of power and strength in the midst of adversity. Jesus knew those depths. He lived in an ocean of constant communion with God.

Most of us choose not to go deep but to live in the shallow end of life. We choose the puddle instead of the ocean.

Now it's confession time: Some pastors say they pray two hours every day. I cannot imagine doing that. I'm tempted to tell them, "Get busy! Stop goofing off!" I confess that I don't have any slacks that are worn out at the knees from prayer.

My prayer life consists of about fifteen minutes each day. As I drive to work in the morning, I pray that God will help me use my time wisely. When I am responding to a telephone call or standing by a hospital bed, I pray that God will give me the right words to say. Before I go to sleep at night, I review in my mind the prayer cards from last Sunday's offering plate, along with the personal and private concerns I have heard, and I lift those concerns up to God. In all, it's perhaps fifteen minutes a day.

There are times, however, when I step out of the puddle and into the ocean. Sometimes in the evening, around nine o'clock, after my last appointment has ended, I walk into the darkened sanctuary. The only illumination in the room is from the cross on the altar, reflecting the golden lights from the parking lot, and the faint glow of the stained glass windows. I kneel by the altar or sit in the front row. I often find my eyes are filled with tears. Some of the tears are for my own sin and shortcomings. Some of the tears come when I read the prayer cards from Sunday morning, where members have poured out their hearts. In the midst of my tears I sense that God is crying too—that God hears these prayers for broken marriages, broken hopes, broken bodies, and broken dreams. There in the night I'm in the ocean, surrounded by the presence of God.

I have an invitation for you. Move from the puddle to the ocean. Allow God to hold you, and mold you, and empower you.

Committed to Christ begins by inviting you to make a commitment to grow at least one step this year in your prayer life. The program begins with prayer, because if you're going to have a personal relationship with the Lord it is going to begin with prayer.

The words of Jesus in Matthew go right to the heart of what prayer is all about:

> When you pray, do not be like the hypocrites! They love to stand up and pray in the houses of worship and on the street corners, so that everyone will see them. I assure you, they have already been paid in full. But when you pray, go to your room, close the door, and pray to your Father, who is unseen. And your Father, who sees what you do in private, will reward you. When you pray, do not use a lot of meaningless words, as the pagans do, who think that their gods will hear them because their prayers are long. Do not be like them. (Matthew 6:5–8a GNT)

Let those words soak in a minute: "When you pray, do not use a lot of meaningless words . . ."

Jesus is teaching that prayer is a very natural and simple thing to do—as natural and simple as talking with your best friend, or eating or sleeping or breathing. Prayer is not a complicated and difficult thing to do at all.

I wonder if that is a message you need to hear this morning: that prayer is as simple and natural as talking to a friend. I wonder what kind of a difference that truth might make in your life.

Richard Foster, in his book on prayer, puts it this way:

> What I am trying to say is that God receives us just as we are and accepts our prayers just as they are. In the same way that a small child cannot draw a bad picture so a child of God cannot offer a bad prayer. So we are brought to the most basic, the most primary form of prayer: Simple Prayer. . . . Like children before a loving father, we open our hearts and make our requests. We do not try to sort things out, the good from the bad. We simply and unpretentiously share our concerns and make our petitions. We tell God, for example, how frustrated we are with the co-worker at the office or the neighbor down the street. We ask for food, favorable weather, and good health.[7]

And then pay attention to these last few words:

Simple Prayer involves ordinary people bringing ordinary concerns to a loving and compassionate Father. There is no pretense in Simple Prayer. We do not pretend to be more holy, more pure, or more saintly than we actually are. We do not try to conceal our conflicting and contradictory motives from God—or ourselves. And in this posture we pour out our heart to the God who is greater than our heart and who knows all things.[8]

Do you understand what this means? *You* can have a prayer life too. Whoever you are, however simple and unsophisticated you think you might be, however "out of touch" you might feel when it comes to religious things, this could be the beginning of an absolutely wonderful life for you. You don't have to carry the burdens of your work, family, health, and finances all by yourself anymore. God would love to help you deal with them on a daily basis. God would love to open up for you closed doors and dead-end roads, leading you in a way that is full of promise and joy.

You don't need to lie awake at night, worrying about all your problems. God would love to take that load off your shoulders and let you get a good night's rest, resulting in a peaceful life.

It's a shame that so many of us go it alone in life, isn't it? It's a shame that we try to handle everything all by ourselves. Even if we struggle and fret and worry and get upset, our Lord is close by and more than anything would love to help us , if we would just give the Lord a chance.

* * *

I remember clearly the day my father died. He lay on his deathbed in the hospital. Dad knew, Mom knew, the family knew, and the doctors knew that my father would never leave the hospital. The day finally came when Dad was unable to move, smile, or talk. However, he could see, and I could tell by the expression in his eyes that he was aware of me and understood what I was saying.

My mother stepped out of the room for a quick trip to the cafeteria. I knelt by my father's bed and held his hand. Dad and I stared into each other's eyes, and I told him my memories of so many things we had done together. I talked about camping trips, fishing trips, projects we had worked on together when I was growing up, and the way he forgave me when I totaled the family car (twice). I talked about the church building committee we both served on and about how beautiful the worship room would be when the stained glass windows were installed. I told Dad that I loved him. I recited aloud Scriptures that I had memorized, including John 3:16, Romans 8:28, Psalm 23, and John 14.

Holding Dad's hand, looking into his eyes, I prayed out loud:

Dear Jesus, thank you for my Daddy. Thank you for making him such a good father. Thank you for his love, forgiveness, and wisdom. Thank you for his baptism and for forgiving his sins. Thank you for making a home for him in heaven. Lord, as Dad lies here with one foot on earth and one foot in heaven, give him such peace inside that you are in control. Guide him on his journey from earth to heaven. Thank you, Jesus, for never leaving my Daddy alone. Amen.

With tears in my eyes, I reminded my father not to be afraid. I told him that we would be okay. I told him that surely his mother and father were standing at the gates of heaven, waiting anxiously for him. I even suggested that his childhood pet, a little Boston terrier, surely must be standing by their side. I said, "I love you, Dad." My mother returned to the room, kissed him, held his hand, and said, "I love you."

Dad knew we were both there. It wasn't long before his breathing began to slow down. Ten, then seven, then five breaths a minute. Then three breaths, and then he was still.

How different the day of my father's death would have been if I did not believe in prayer. Do you have a prayer life that gives you strength in tough times?

*   *   *

We continue in Matthew 6, where Jesus gives an example of prayer. It's the prayer we have come to call the Lord's Prayer. The form most of us use today is:

Our Father, who art in heaven, hallowed be thy name. Thy kingdom come, thy will be done on earth as it is in heaven. Give us this day our daily bread. And forgive us our trespasses, as we forgive those who trespass against us. And lead us not into temptation, but deliver us from evil. For thine is the kingdom, and the power, and the glory, forever. Amen.

In this prayer there are sixty-seven words. Do you know how many of those words have just one syllable? Fifty! Isn't it interesting that when Jesus taught us to pray, he taught us to use one-syllable words?

Prayer, according to Jesus, does not have to be fancy, sophisticated, or impressive. Do you know why? Because God is down-to-earth, loving, and personable, and he wants to have that kind of relationship with you and me. God cares about *you*!

A few years ago a group of about a dozen young people visited the church where I was pastor. They were members of a youth group from a church that we had helped start in Russia. They came to visit, along with their pastor. As the Russian young people interacted with our local youth group, there were some awkward moments. Then someone found a basketball. Within minutes, Russians and Americans were shooting hoops in our fellowship hall. It was amazing; you couldn't tell "them" from "us."

The mayor stopped by and presented each Russian youth with a T-shirt from the city. As we all stood holding hands in a prayer circle, I remembered what I had thought of Russians growing up. They were the enemy. When I had lived in Houston, Texas, during the Cuban missile crisis, we had nuclear bomb drills. The teacher would have us hide under our school desks, practicing what we would do if the Russian missiles were launched from Cuba. Years later, watching the youth playing basketball together, it dawned on me that even back in the 1960s, praying the "Our Father" included these Russian youth, too. Perhaps, before my eyes, I was seeing God's answer to my parents' nightly prayer for peace.

Have you ever had friends who talked to you only when they wanted something, who acted as if you didn't exist the rest of the time, who warmed up to you when they needed to borrow your class notes or your lawn mower or your money?

Many of us seem to treat God like that. We believe, but we ignore God most of the time. All that changes when we need something and suddenly we pray as if we were close friends of the Lord. These types of prayers are empty, stagnant, lifeless, and stale.

How can we, if we pray so rarely, expect to have a vibrant, thriving relationship with the Lord? As weak as we are—so prone to wander away from God and so prone to distraction—we should be on our knees twenty-three hours a day, just to find the strength to be faithful that one remaining hour of the day.

How is your prayer life? Are you opening yourself up to God daily, or are you approaching God only when you have a shopping list of needs? Do you listen to Christian radio stations? Do you read your church's prayer list each night before you fall asleep? Do you pray for your mother, father, aunts, uncles, brothers, sisters, spouse, and children? Do you remember them and their needs in your prayers to the Lord? Do you end each day praying, "Here I am Lord. I am yours. Speak, Lord, your servant is listening."? Do you begin each day praying, "Lord, how can I best serve you today? Mold me. Shape me. Use me."

Let prayer become a regular habit. Set a time each day to pray, perhaps when you first get up, in the shower, driving to school, during your lunch break, or just before you fall asleep. Whatever time you choose, let that be a holy time; a holy place where you meet alone with God; a place where you reach up to God and allow God to reach down to you.

Dr. Tammy Garrison tells the story of a Haitian woman named Simone Gustave. When they met, Simone had been a hospital patient for eight years, suffering from leprosy. Before getting treatment, she had lost the first two joints on all her fingers, and her face was horribly disfigured. But she did not lose her ability to pray. Here is one of her prayers:

Here I sit, propped up with pillows on my bed in the corner of the ward, my home for eight years now.

What do I do here all day? Someone asked me that this afternoon. Maybe they think I get bored or lonely. But how could I, when you are here with me, Lord? You are my life and you give me everything. The light that streams in from the window behind me, the flowers on my nightstand, the wheelchair by my bed and the special shoes that help me get around . . . the nuns and doctors and nurses who take care of me, all of this comes from you, good Lord.

And so with you I sing. I pray. I talk to my neighbors. I watch the people passing in the corridor.

Sometimes my son is there, coming to visit me. Sometimes I spot groups of visitors who come to see the clinic. . . . Sometimes I see the outpatients who have come for treatment. . . . So as I sit here I ask you: Bless them all, good Lord. I pray for all my brothers and sisters, for those in Haiti, and those in all other countries. I pray for the people who have helped me by helping this clinic.

Keep watching over Simone Gustave, Lord. Keep her strong. Give her courage. Mother Mary, pray for me. Holy Spirit, direct me and watch over me. Bless me and purify me. Thank you God. You do all this for Simone Gustave.[9]

What an amazing spirit Simone has. She has lost much, but in some ways she has so much more than I do. What a simple and amazing prayer life. Simone does what Jesus taught: "When you pray, do not use a lot of meaningless words."

God cares not only about you, but also about your neighbors. A member of my church invited her Sunday school class to pray for six minutes a day for six days for six neighbors. What would happen in your life if for the next six days you prayed six minutes a day for six neighbors?

Who might these neighbors be? Perhaps they would be the single mom in the apartment next door; the family in the mobile home next to yours; the person who stands next to you at work; the student who sits next to you; or the teammate you play soccer with.

What would you pray for? Another member of my church taught me to pray for five blessings, making up the word *BLESS*:

Body (health, protection)
Labor (work, income, security)
Emotional (joy, peace, hope)
Social (love, marriage, family, friends)
Spiritual (salvation, faith, grace)

To pray, you don't need fancy words. You don't need proper grammar. You don't need pious clichés. You don't need proper sentence structure. You don't need words that flow poetically. All you need is a heart that loves God and a human need that asks to be addressed.

If you'll pray that way—from your heart, expressing to the Lord whatever you want to share—you can be assured that the Lord will hear your prayer. The Lord is wonderful, far more than most of us would ever guess. The Lord is close to all of us all the time, far closer than most of us would begin to imagine. Prayer is the way we can be in touch with the Lord and the Lord in touch with us.

God does not always answer our prayers the way we want them answered. I do not know why. What I do know is that God hears your prayers. God cares about you. I have witnessed God performing miracles on broken hearts, broken lives, broken marriages, and broken bodies. I have witnessed sin forgiven, fear turned into faith, and hate turned into love. I know that whatever may come, God will walk with you every step of the journey, and that is why we should keep on praying and never lose heart.

Why make prayer difficult? Simply pray!

O Lord, is it true that you listen when we pray? Could it be true that you know each of us by name? Could it be true that you care for each of us? Could it be true that you care enough to show us the way to live a full and abundant life? O Lord, we hope it's true. In the weeks ahead, teach us how to pray. Amen.

PRAYER MADE EASY

Olu Brown

A well-known office supply store has a popular marketing tool
called the "easy button." It sends a clear message that dealing
with the employees, locating items, and checking out at the register
should be easy for the customer. I am glad the business world has
finally discovered that in our fast-paced, ever-changing lives, people
need fewer steps, less process, and simpler systems. However, I am
not sure if this is the case in the spiritual world, especially when it
comes to prayer.

My personal struggle is that I always have had difficulty main-
taining a consistent and fruitful prayer life. I now realize the barrier is
within me: all my crazy, preprogrammed, learned expectations con-
cerning prayer. I believe I have been making prayer too difficult and not
"easy."

In Mark 8, Jesus fed more than five thousand people with a meal
the size of an appetizer at your favorite restaurant. He lifted the appetizer to God and offered a prayer that was simple and straight to the
point. No frills! He didn't go to a special place, wear fancy clothes, or

recite a unique liturgy. He said what was on his mind and became the catalyst for one of the greatest miracles of all time.

For me, this example of prayer is truly a relief—no frills, just genuine prayer. My hope for you is that you don't develop a prayer life with thousands of steps or inflexible rules. Keep prayer easy, and see God's power revealed.

Olu Brown, the lead pastor of Impact Church in downtown Atlanta, Georgia, has helped make Impact one of the fastest growing new churches in America. Impact Church is a multicultural gathering of people who are committed to sharing the love of Christ with the world and doing church differently.

2.
READING THE
BIBLE DAILY

The theologian Albert Outler once was asked, "What is the Bible?" This was his response:

> The word means *book*. For Christians, this is the book that is a unique book of many books, with many kinds of literature: saga, history, law, poetry, prophecy, with occasional pieces like Esther, Ruth, Jonah, and Job; one Gospel in four versions, a slice of early church history, a collection of epistles, and an arousing but bewildering climax. It is one coherent narrative from Genesis to Revelation. It is the story of what God has been doing and will always be doing on earth for his people. It is the story of what he has designed us for, and what he rightfully expects from us. It is the story of what we can count on from God: covenant making and covenant keeping on his part; covenant making and covenant breaking on our side. It is a book that helps us become truly human.[10]

Did you hear that? It is the story of what God has designed us for, and what God rightfully expects from us. It is a book that helps us become truly human.

I wonder what would have to change in your life for you to allow the Bible to help you become all that God wants you to become? I wonder what would have to happen for you to learn how to listen to the words of Scripture, to accept the words of Scripture, and to live out the teachings of Scripture?

Are you ready for that kind of journey?

*　　*　　*

At the age of forty, Erik Weihenmayer is a world-class athlete: acrobatic skydiver, long-distance biker, marathon runner, skier, mountaineer, ice climber, and rock climber. Mountain climbing is his specialty. As a matter of fact, he has climbed all the "Seven Summits," the highest mountain on each of the seven continents. The peaks he has conquered include Mt. McKinley, Yosemite's El Capitan, Mt. Kilimanjaro, Argentina's Aconcagua, and Mt. Everest in Tibet. In 2008 he stood atop the Carstensz Pyramid, the tallest mountain in Australasia.

There is something else about Eric you need to know. Erik suffers from a degenerative eye disease. By the time he was thirteen he was totally blind. All his climbs have been without the benefit of eyesight. Erik is a blind mountain-climber.[11]

You are probably wondering, "How can a blind person climb any mountain, much less the highest mountains on all seven continents?" If you asked Erik, he would respond, "I have learned to listen well." Eric listens to a bell tied to the climber in front of him. He listens to his climbing partners, who shout back instructions to him such as "Drop-off, two feet to your right!" He listens to the sound of his pick jabbing the ice, so he knows whether his next step will be secure or not. For Erik, being a good listener is a matter of life and death.

According to the Bible, the same is true for us, too. Being a good listener is a matter of life and death.

When I first began my personal journey with Christ, reading the Bible for the first time as an adult, I simply fell in love with the book of James. In the New Testament that I carried, I underlined the entire book of James. This letter is only about five pages long, but in its words

I found great wisdom to begin my journey toward discipleship. In James 1:19-25, we read,

> My dear brothers and sisters, take note of this: Everyone should be quick to listen, slow to speak and slow to become angry, because human anger does not produce the righteousness that God desires. Therefore, get rid of all moral filth and the evil that is so prevalent and humbly accept the word planted in you, which can save you. Do not merely listen to the word, and so deceive yourselves. Do what it says. Anyone who listens to the word but does not do what it says is like someone who looks at his face in a mirror and, after looking at himself, goes away and immediately forgets what he looks like. But whoever looks intently into the perfect law that gives freedom, and continues in it—not forgetting what they have heard, but doing it—they will be blessed in what they do. (NIV)

In this brief passage, James is offering a challenge for us to take God's word seriously enough that it changes our behavior. James invites us to listen to God's word, to accept the truth of what it reveals, and to change our behavior accordingly.

It's not easy to listen to God's word. How often do you hear the Bible read from the pulpit or read it yourself, but the words don't sink in? It's hard to listen. It's hard to let the words sink in. Here's a story that illustrates this:

> A hundred years ago, when the telegraph was the fastest method of long-distance communication, a young man applied for a job as a Morse code operator. In response to an ad in the newspaper, he went to the office to apply for the job. When he arrived he entered a large, busy room filled with noise and clatter, including the sound of a telegraph in the background. A sign on the receptionist's desk instructed job applicants to fill out a form and wait until they were summoned to enter the inner office.
>
> The young man filled out his form and sat down in the waiting area with seven other applicants. After a few minutes, the young man stood up and walked into the inner office. Naturally the other applicants perked up, wondering what was going on. Soon the employer escorted the young man out of the office and said to the other applicants, "Thank you for applying, but the job has just been filled."
>
> The other applicants began grumbling, and one spoke up, saying, "Wait a minute, I don't understand. We never got a chance to be interviewed. And to top it off, this guy comes in last and you hire him.

That's not fair!"

The employer said, "I'm sorry you feel that way. You all had the same opportunity. During the last several minutes while you've been sitting here, didn't you hear the telegraph key clicking? It was sending the following words in Morse code: 'If you understand this message, then come right in. The job is yours.' None of you heard it or understood it. This young man did. The job is his!"[12]

Far too often, we let the words of the Bible drift in one ear and float out the other. The first chapter of James makes it clear: Don't do that! James writes that not only do we need to listen but we also need to accept the truth of what the Scripture reveals to us.

*   *   *

When I was a teenager growing up in Russellville, Arkansas, my pastor, Charles Ramsay, told a story one Sunday that got my attention.[13] It was a sad story about a father and son who were having communication problems. As the boy neared his sixteenth birthday, he began a relentless quest to have his parents buy him a new car. He launched a constant barrage of requests and pressured them to give in.

On his sixteenth birthday, as the son turned off his alarm clock he noticed a small giftwrapped box on his bedside table. He realized it was just the right size to hold the owner's manual and a set of keys for a new car. His hopes were raised when he glanced at the note his father had attached to the package: *Son, look carefully inside. You will find everything you've been wishing for.*

The boy tore open the box, looked inside, and could not believe what he saw. His parents had given him a Bible, not a car. Angry and frustrated, he tossed the Bible in the corner of his bedroom and stormed out of the house. He resolved that he would never listen to his parents again and would find a way to move out of their house as soon as possible. The relationship at home turned ugly, and although the parents repeatedly tried to reach out to their son, he ignored them.

Years later, now a father himself, the same man found himself cleaning out his parents' old home, preparing to settle their estate. Boxing up things from his old bedroom, he came across the Bible his parents had given him for his sixteenth birthday. As he tossed the Bible into the box, a slip of paper stuck out from the edge of the pages. Reaching for it, he discovered a check from his parents dated on his sixteenth birthday, in an amount more than enough to purchase a brand-new car. Holding the check, he remembered his father's note: *Son, look carefully inside. You will find everything you've been wishing for.*

It is hard to listen. It is hard to let words sink in. But we always need to listen, as James writes, for the Word of God. We must listen with the intensity of Erik Weihenmayer, the blind adventurer who has summited the highest peak on every continent, including Everest. Erik listens to the bells on the ropes, to the words of his fellow climbers, and the sound of his pick hitting the ice. Erik listens carefully because his life depends on it. We need to be listening to the words of Scripture as if our life depends on it, because indeed it does.

*   *   *

One pastor tells the story of a man who was driving down a road. A woman drove toward him from the opposite direction. As they passed each other, the woman leaned out her car window and yelled, "Pig!" The man, incensed, leaned out his window and yelled back at her.

They each continued on their way. As the man rounded the next curve, he crashed into a huge pig that was standing in the middle of the road. The man was unhurt, but his car was a total wreck.

The man heard her message but did not understand or accept it. When it comes to the Bible, we not only need to hear God's word but to understand it and accept it as valid and important for our daily lives.

*   *   *

It is said that John Bunyan, author of *Pilgrim's Progress*, wrote these words inside the front cover of his Bible: *This book will keep you from sin, or sin will keep you from this book.*

It's a sad fact: When sin has control of our lives and we need the Bible the most, those are the times when we are least likely to read it. Why is that? I think sometimes we are not ready to handle the truth. We fall into sinful patterns. We avoid the subject of religion altogether. And we find ways to skip attending worship and reading the Bible. The resources that can help lift us out of the "pit" are the very things we shy away from. In Paul's second letter to Timothy, we read:

> You have been taught the Holy Scriptures from childhood, and they have given you the wisdom to receive the salvation that comes by trusting in Christ Jesus. All Scripture is inspired by God and is useful to teach us what is true and to make us realize what is wrong in our lives. It corrects us when we are wrong and teaches us to do what is right. God uses it to prepare and equip his people to do every good work. (2 Timothy 3:15-17 NLT)

We are not simply invited to read the Bible; we are invited to *accept* its teachings. The Bible teaches us: Remember the Sabbath day and keep it holy. Honor your father and your mother. You shall not commit adultery. You shall not steal. You shall not bear false witness against your neighbor. You shall not covet your neighbor's house, wife, or anything that belongs to your neighbor. When the Bible teaches us, we are not to argue nor look for loopholes. Instead, we are to accept what we read in the Word of God.

*   *   *

James writes that indeed we are to listen and accept what we read in the Bible. He also says we should have *behavior that matches*—that we should obey what we read in the Scriptures.

Isn't it amazing how we have the ability to behave in patterns that contradict our knowledge? We can hear words from our doctor, even accept those words as true, and yet never let them change our behavior.

This week, our invitation in Committed to Christ: Six Weeks to a Generous Life is not simply to clock in hours of reading the Bible but also to let the words of that holy and sacred book change our behavior. Are you ready not only to read, but to obey?

One suggestion: If you are really serious about this invitation, find someone you trust and make yourself accountable to that person. Say to your trusted friend, "I've got a problem. My constant _____ is hurting my relationship with God. Will you keep me accountable? Will you keep me honest on this?"

We all know that eventually we will have to answer to God about our lives, but that seems like a long way off. If, however, we know that this week we will have to look a friend in the eye and answer for our behavior, that may give us the resolve to sin less and live a more holy life.

I remember well when one such friend and I decided to hold each other accountable. We both had a short list of sinful behaviors we were ready to change but were unable to change on our own. My friend and I held each other accountable. We heard each other's confessions. We prayed for each other. To help remember our shared covenant, I wore my watch on the opposite wrist, carried my billfold in a different pocket, and wore a cross under my shirt so the cold metal of the cross would remind me of the promises I had made to the Lord.

Set aside a regular time each day to spend at least fifteen minutes reading the Bible. Find a quiet place at home, work, or school. Let that place become holy ground for you and the Lord as you open the sacred pages and invite the Lord to speak. Invite the Lord to grow inside you and to fill you until you learn to live faithfully, in harmony with the words of the Bible.

There are many Christians who underline and mark the pages of the Bible. May there be as many Christians who allow the Bible to make a positive mark on their lives.

In James's letter, he says that we become motivated to change by looking into the mirror of God's word. He writes: "Those who hear but don't do the word are like those who look at their faces in a mirror. They look at themselves, walk away, and immediately forget what they were like" James 1:23-24 (CEB).

Normally, people look in a mirror for a reason. If they see their hair is out of place, they fix it. If they see a piece of lettuce between their teeth, they remove it. If they see that they cut themselves shaving, they stop the bleeding.

When you look into the Bible and see something that needs to be fixed, don't turn away. Ask God for the courage, guidance, and strength to change.

* * *

Are you ready to grow one or more steps in your commitment to read the Bible daily? Are you ready to live by its words?

- If you don't have a Bible, make a commitment today to buy one.
- If you have a Bible but it is still in the box, make a commitment today to take it out and use it.
- If you have a Bible but it just gathers dust on your bedside table, make a commitment today to dust if off every Sunday morning and read the Scriptures as you prepare to attend worship.
- If you have developed the holy habit of reading the Bible only on Sunday mornings, make a commitment to read it daily.
- If you already have a daily Bible-reading habit, make a commitment to read systematically instead of randomly. You might consider reading the New Testament from front to back, or using a schedule to read the entire Bible in one, two, or three years.
- If you currently read the Bible alone, make a commitment to be part of a Bible study group that meets regularly, to better understand what you read.

No matter what your level of commitment, let the words sink in. Live them. Obey them. Allow God to bless your life so it will be a holy blessing to others.

Lord, what would you have us read? How would you have us use our time? What are the priorities? We have time to read the news online. We have time to read Newsweek, Time, O, *and* Southern Living. *We have time to read novels on our iPads. Lord, do you want us to read the Bible? Is it worth our time? You've given us 10,000 minutes each week; how many of those minutes should we spend reading the Bible? Are Bible study groups worth our time? Where would you use our energies? Help us, Lord, to know what you would have us do.*

Lord, we thank you for the Bible. We thank you for the way you teach us. We thank you for the great stories in it, about your will for our lives. Lord, you know that many of us are spiritually malnourished because we have not been feasting on your Word. Create a hunger within us for this Bible. Help us to be a church, built and founded upon this Bible. Amen.

God's
Measuring Stick

James W. Moore

Some years ago, there was a great professor at Centenary College, Dean R. E. Smith, a very distinctive-looking man who wore a black patch over one eye. Dean Smith was a saintly man, a brilliant scholar, an outstanding communicator, a true friend to his students, and a legend in his own time.

In one of his most famous lectures, Dean Smith spoke to his students about how we discover truth and how we determine what is genuine and authentic. After some discussion, Dean Smith suddenly asked, "How wide is my desk?" The students would look at the desk and then make their best guesses. A variety of answers would ring out.

"I think it's about 72 inches wide."

"No, I believe it's more like 68 inches wide."

"Looks like 75 to me."

"I'm going to guess 74 inches."

Then some wise guy from the back of the room would say, "71 and 5/16?" and everyone would laugh.

Then Dean Smith would say, "Those are all pretty good guesses, but one of them is more nearly true than the others. Now, how do we determine which one is most accurate? How do we decide which answer is most nearly right?"

There would be complete silence for a moment in the classroom, and then someone would ask tentatively, "Get a measuring stick?"

"That's right," Dean Smith would say. "To determine which one is closest to the truth, we have to get a measuring stick and measure it!"

Then he would go to the blackboard. He would take a piece of chalk, and, in silence, draw the outline of a cross. With the chalk, he would trace over and over the outline of the cross, letting it dramatically sink into the hearts and minds of those students.

Then he would stand back, point to that cross, and say, "There's your measuring stick! There's your measuring stick for truth!"

With the Bible comes God's encouraging promise: Here's your compass. Here's your guiding light. Here's your measuring stick for truth.

Study the Bible. Memorize its key verses. Get the Scriptures inside of you. Write them on your heart. Immerse yourselves in the Bible. Learn the key themes of the Bible. And the Bible will be your measuring stick to show you what is true and right and good.

James W. Moore, popular speaker and preacher, has written more than forty books, including Yes, Lord, I Have Sinned, But I Have Several Excellent Excuses; God Was Here, and I Was Out to Lunch; When Grief Breaks Your Heart; *and* There's a Hole in Your Soul That Only God Can Fill. *He and his wife, June, live in Fairview, Texas.*

*Reprinted from James W. Moore, *Standing on the Promises or Sitting on the Premises?* Nashville: Abingdon Press, 1995, pp. 113–15.

3.
LET US GO TO THE HOUSE OF THE LORD

Have you ever heard the phrase "preaching to the choir"? It happens when preachers forget that most of their audiences each week are the faithful saints, not unrepentant sinners. In this chapter, if I were to fuss at you for not attending worship I would most likely be preaching to the choir, because the odds are that you are a regular worship attender, and in fact may be inside a church building at this very moment.

A couple of years ago when I conducted a statistical study of my congregation's worship attendance, we had an average attendance of slightly more than 500. On a typical Sunday 75% of the attendees were members, 21% were continuing guests, and 4% were first-time worship guests. In that young congregation, among the resident members we found that 76% attended four or more times a month, 20% attended fewer than four times a month, and about 4% never attended worship. While those numbers may be typical for new churches, among resident members of older churches the typical pattern seems to be that about 33% attend four or more times a month, 33% attend fewer than four times a month, and 33% never attend.

I suspect that, as a reader of this study book, you are already among the group that attends worship on a rather frequent basis. You, most likely, already have a great commitment to the first and fourth commandments: "Remember the Sabbath day and keep it holy" and "I am the Lord your God, you shall have no other gods before me." Perhaps, then, the challenge before us is not so much a challenge of quantity as of quality.

Are you ready to step up and be passionate about worship as a true priority in your life?

On this week's commitment card, most of us may quickly check, without hesitation, "I will attend worship three or four times a month" and perhaps even check "As my health permits, I will never miss worship." The more challenging area may be the fine print at the bottom of the worship commitment card that reads:

> Worship will be a priority in my life, growing to include the following: I will be passionate about worship as a true priority in my life. Bad weather, sports, or holidays will not keep me from attending worship. I will prepare the day before, so that I can arrive at worship without last-minute rushing. I will warmly greet those who sit around me. I will surround my family and friends with worship. Through worship I will seek to find strength, power, and direction to face the week.

James Moore tells the story of a young Catholic priest who finished his theological training and was appointed to serve a parish in Loveland, Colorado.[14] The young priest was excited to celebrate his first mass and wanted everything to be perfect. He even put fresh water in the bowl by the front door, so worshipers could dip their fingers in and make the sign of the cross upon entering for worship. On his first Sunday morning, the priest anxiously waited, watching the parking lot entrance from his study window. He was thrilled to see so many cars enter the parking lot. "Wow," he said out loud, "We're going to have a packed house today!" However, just a few minutes later, when he walked into the sanctuary to begin the mass, he was stunned to see that only seventeen people were there. He was stunned, disappointed, and mystified. He had seen the line of cars entering the parking lot, but where were all those people? The next Sunday, he was amazed to find that the same thing happened! On the third Sunday, the priest decided to get to the bottom of it. Instead of watching from his study window, he stood at the entrance to the building. Immediately the mystery was solved. Sure enough, a large number of cars entered the parking lot and soon a large number of people entered the building. However, instead of coming all the way in and taking a seat, the people stepped in just far enough to dip their fingers in the holy water and make the sign of the cross, then scurried out of the church, got back in their cars, and drove off to other pursuits.

It is a sad image: people coming in just far enough to touch the holy water. It is a sad commentary on far too many of our churches. Across this nation, there are millions who want to come just far enough into the church to get a sprinkling of religion, just far enough to get their names on the books, but not far enough to give their hearts and souls to the cause of Christ.

*   *   *

If we are attending worship every Sunday to be entertained, if we are not striving to live a holy life, if our hearts are not changing, if we are not trying to be a fully devoted disciple—then we've missed the point. The point isn't just to show up on Sunday, but through worship to grow into fully devoted disciples of Jesus Christ, who then help others become disciples too.

It seems that there are many churchgoers who try to confine God to Sunday morning. You might say they just want to give God one hour a week and that's it! These people are saying, in effect, "Forget this commitment business. I don't want to bother with that. Look, let's just occasionally come to church on Sunday morning, listen to some great music, and leave it at that. I'm not a bad person. I'm not an evil person. I just don't want to make such a big deal out of all this."

I understand those feelings. However, I have to be honest with you. The journey toward becoming a deeply devoted disciple is not just an option; it is an expectation the Lord has of everyone who seeks to be a Christian, a follower of Christ, a disciple. Our Lord does indeed care about how we live and whether or not we attend worship each week.

Jesus' first sermon can be found in Matthew 5, 6, and 7. In that sermon, Jesus lays out a pretty stiff set of expectations—powerful words about important issues such as marriage, forgiveness, and relationships. Near the end of his remarks, he makes the point that if you are indeed a faithful follower, it will be evident in the way you live. Are you a faithful disciple? What kind of fruit are you producing? Jesus said,

> "You can identify a tree by its fruit. You don't pick grapes from thorn bushes, or figs from thistles. A healthy tree produces good fruit, and an unhealthy tree produces bad fruit. . . . So every tree that does not produce good fruit is chopped down and thrown into the fire. The way to identify a tree or a person is by the kind of fruit that is produced." (Matthew 7:16-20 LNT)

*   *   *

Isaiah 61:3 has another powerful image for us today: We might become "oaks of righteousness. The planting of the LORD, that he may be glorified" (KJV).

There is an old poster in the archives of Hendrix College in Conway, Arkansas. The poster advertises Hendrix College about the time of its 100th anniversary. On the poster, underneath the image of a big oak tree, appears this slogan: *It takes 30 days to grow a squash. It takes 100 years to grow a mighty oak.*

When my wife and I built our current home back in 1994, we bought a bundle of hardwood seedlings from the Arkansas Forestry Commission. The little trees looked pitiful. They were no thicker than a pencil, and not much taller either. Today, those trees are no longer pencil-thick. They are fifty feet tall and eighteen inches thick, well on their way to becoming mighty oak trees.

Are you on your way to becoming a mighty oak of God, a mighty woman of God, a mighty man of God?

Think with me. What kind of a mighty oak of God would you become if you *never* missed worship—if you spent at least fifty-two hours a year, one hour a week, offering praise to God and receiving forgiveness, comfort, guidance, and strength from the Lord? Would that help you grow into a mighty oak of God?

Think with me. What kind of a mighty oak of God would you become if you spent fifteen minutes in prayer every day, setting that time aside for the Lord, holding your Bible, reading those holy words, letting them sink in, lifting your prayers to God, and listening to the word of God? Would that help you begin to grow into a mighty oak of God?

Think with me. What kind of mighty oak of God would you become if witnessing and inviting became a part of your daily life? What kind of mighty oak of God would you become if you could look around the room on Sunday and count ten, twenty, even fifty people who were active participants because of your invitation and witness?

Think with me. What kind of mighty oak of God would you become if you were generous, financially supporting the ministries of your church? Did you know that it costs thousands of dollars a year to keep the doors open at your church and keep the building clean, make the monthly mortgage payment, buy Sunday school literature, have children's and youth ministries, supply a fair share of the support for missionaries around the world, fund campus ministries, and provide a pension for retired pastors and their survivors? Do you spend more money renting movies, paying for a cell phone, and eating out than you give to the Lord? Do you waste more money each week than you typically give on Sunday morning? What kind of mighty oak of God would you become if you generously supported the Sunday offering at your church?

Think with me. What kind of mighty oak of God would you become if you gave your time to serve in Jesus' name—volunteering in the nursery, mowing the church lawn, visiting worship guests in their homes, helping with the hospital ministry, caring for homebound members, providing music in worship, or acting as adult counselor for youth ministry? What kind of mighty oak of God would you become if you served the Lord through the United Way agencies in your county, or gave your time to serve foreign missions through your church? What kind of mighty oak of God would you become if you had blisters on your hands from serving in Jesus' name?

Over the next few weeks, your church will be inviting you to reengage in the journey toward Christian perfection. Are you ready?

Is attendance at worship each week a priority for you? Are you passionate about attending worship? Do you simply attend, or do you open your heart to the presence of God during worship?

To make worship a priority, how will you need to change? What will have to change in your heart? What will have to change at your home? What will have to change at work? What will have to change in your use of time?

I love an old story that comes from the mission field. The offering plate was being passed down the row of chairs one Sunday. A new convert didn't have any money to place in the offering, so he simply put the plate on the floor and stood in it, offering himself to the Lord.

Are you ready to offer yourself to the Lord this week in worship? By the power of God, your future can be different from your past. Are you ready for the journey?

Is today the day to reengage with the Lord? Is today the day to take the next step?

Lord, I have a hunger for worship to become the highlight of my every week. I have a hunger to open my heart to your presence during worship. Lord, help me discover ways to make worship a true priority in my life. Remind me each week, Lord, to come to worship prepared, without last-minute rushing. Through worship, give me the strength, power, and guidance to face the week ahead. Amen.

FAITHFUL
WORSHIP ATTENDANCE

Rick Bezet

A t New Life Church, just after we built our first building in Conway, Arkansas, a very distinguished-looking man approached me
after the service with red eyes, evidently from crying. Standing behind
him were his wife and two children. With quivering lips, the man told
me that this was his family's first visit to our church and that he loved
it, but that he had a serious question: "Can this church accept a man like
me, who shoved his wife into the wall last week while his kids were
watching? Can the church allow a person who struggles with anger to
come?" His wife's eyes were silently saying, "Please say yes." It took
a lot of courage for this man to approach me.

I told him that God is able to heal his anger as though it were never
there and even to establish him as a leader who can help other families.
This has actually become true, and this family serves faithfully in our
small group ministry and in welcoming people into our foyer during
weekend services.

This man made an adjustment that some people never make. That
first day he came in need; he was a "consumer." He needed something

we could offer to him, an encounter with a real Savior. He could have kept coming back to church, always looking for another way Jesus could meet his needs, but instead he became a "contributor" and gave to others.

Rick Bezet is the founder and lead pastor of New Life Church in Central Arkansas. NLC was America's fastest growing church in 2009, according to Outreach Magazine. *Rick is also a founding board member and overseer of the Association of Related Churches, a nationwide church-planting organization.*

4.
You Shall Be My Witnesses

A longtime pastor and evangelist once told of going through his mother's things after she died in 2010. There was a formal will that her attorney had prepared years ago, but in the bedside table at the nursing home, he found a handwritten last will and testament.

This handwritten will was different from the original. At first he thought of just setting it aside, but his daughter objected. "Daddy, no," she told him. "It doesn't matter what it says; those were Grandma's last wishes. We have to do exactly as she instructed."

And that is what they did. They followed her last wishes.

Did you know that we have Jesus' last words too? They appear in the first chapter of Acts. Jesus and his disciples gathered on the Mount of Olives on the west side of Jerusalem's Kidron Valley. Moments before Jesus ascended into heaven, he said,

> "You don't get to know the time. Timing is the Father's business. What you'll get is the Holy Spirit. And when the Holy Spirit comes on you, you will be able to be my witnesses in Jerusalem, all over

Judea and Samaria, even to the ends of the world" (Acts 1:7-8 *THE MESSAGE*).

What should we do with these last words of Jesus? How should we respond to his command to "be my witnesses"?

I propose to you that the daughter in this story is right: We must do exactly as instructed. We must serve Jesus by being his witnesses.

*   *   *

In the fourth chapter of Colossians, we find advice on witnessing. The Apostle Paul writes, "Live wisely among those who are not Christians, and make the most of every opportunity. Let your conversation be gracious and effective so that you will have the right answer for everyone" (Colossians 4:5-6 NLT).

Paul is suggesting that when witnessing to "those who are not Christians," we should know who they are, how they think, and what their life goals are. We should discover patterns of relating to them in ways that will be positive and not offend them.

Paul is also suggesting that we use "gracious and effective" words that are warm, caring, and kind. When witnessing, we should not relate in a way that puts people down, discredits them, or insults them.

Further, Paul writes that we should "make the most of every opportunity." To me, this phrase reflects the fact that as Christians we have a mission, a task, a purpose. Part of that mission is to grow disciples who in turn will grow new disciples, sharing the story of Jesus Christ and telling the good news of what God has done in Jesus, and all of this should be accomplished in a winsome and invitational way. This task of witnessing is part of who we are as Christians and part of the essence of our faith.

Whether we are a baker, barber, or bricklayer, if Christ lives inside of us, if Christ is the Lord of our lives, then we must share the good news of Jesus Christ. We must bear witness to others. We must "make the most of every opportunity." We must not be offensive. We must not be inappropriate or barge in uninvited. However, we must share our faith with others.

The only question is how and when.

* * *

On Sunday afternoons, if I happen to encounter a sales clerk, I frequently ask, "Do you have to work every Sunday morning, or do you occasionally get to attend worship?" That simple question almost always elicits a friendly conversation and gives me the opportunity to invite that person to attend Sunday evening worship.

My mother was passionate about inviting people to worship. She was the office manager for a poultry supply company, which meant that all the customers had to come to her office to place their orders. After worship on Sundays she would pick up a dozen or so leftover worship bulletins and take them to work with her. Then, on Mondays, she would ask each customer, "How was church yesterday?" If the customer was an active church attender, her simple question introduced a friendly conversation and often began a new Christian friendship. If the customer hesitated or gave some excuse, she would quickly hand them a worship bulletin with the words, "My husband and I really enjoy First Church. Why don't you sit with us next Sunday?"

I have frequently followed my mother's example. I can report dozens of people who became active participants at my church as a result.

Occasionally the Lord presents the opportunity for a more in-depth witness. A friend of mine wears a class ring on his right hand. When he bought that ring in college many years ago, he was given an opportunity to choose the shape displayed on the face of the ring. He chose a small cross.

Years later my friend was on a plane flight, and a woman sat next to him. After they had been in the air for a while, she happened to notice his ring. "Are you some kind of religious person?" she asked. "That cross on your ring must mean you're a Christian or something."

He told her that indeed he was a Christian. She smiled and said, "You know, I used to go to church myself when I was a little girl. But I haven't gone for years. I don't know why. I just haven't."

She went on to say, "Life's been pretty tough for me. I got pregnant when I was fifteen and married when I was sixteen, to a guy who was nine years older than me. We divorced a year later, and I got married again when I was nineteen. I've been married and divorced four times now, to men who beat me and took advantage of me. I don't think marriage is for me."

My friend said, "I'm sorry. I'm so sorry to hear that. What a disappointment that must be for you."

And she continued, "Yeah, it really is. I mean, I think marriage ought to be for life, a sacred thing, you know? That's what the Bible says, doesn't it? But it hasn't been that way for me."

My friend just listened as she continued her story. Then she said something that gave him an opportunity to share his faith in Jesus Christ. She asked, "Do you think going to church could help me?"

And my friend said, "Of course. But even more than that, Jesus Christ can help you. Christ can help you start putting your life back together. You know, the Lord knows who you are, and the Lord is inside of you right now."

Hearing those words, the woman began to cry. "I can't imagine that," she said. "I really can't. Christ is inside of me?"

My friend smiled and said, "Yes, he is. And he is not judging you either. He's there to help you. He's the best friend you'll ever have."

Believe it or not, the two of them prayed together as they sat on that plane. My friend asked the Lord to come into her heart, to make a difference in her life, to help her find a new life and a new beginning for herself. And you know what? As they were walking off the plane, she turned around and said, "There's a church not far from my house, and I think I'll go there next Sunday."

And she did. How do I know? It just so happened that at 10:45 the next Sunday, as my friend was going into worship at his own church, he saw her walk into the lobby.

The point is this: We don't have to force ourselves on strangers. God is always opening doors for us to be witnesses. Maybe it will happen tomorrow morning in the carpool, maybe on the Internet tonight, maybe sitting next to a stranger on your next flight, maybe with a member of your own family tomorrow. But make no mistake about it: God will open doors for you to be a witness.

Will you realize when God opens that door? Will you speak for God when it happens?

*   *   *

Some years ago, at the end of a seminar, a college professor asked if there were any other questions. Sure enough, a "smart guy" in the back of the room held up his hand and said half-jokingly, "I have a question. What is the meaning of life?"

Of course, everyone laughed. They knew it was an impossible question and that the student was teasing.

But the professor, well into his seventies, didn't laugh. He reached into his pocket and pulled out a little round object. It was a very small mirror, no bigger than a quarter. Then the professor said,

> When I was a small child, during the war, we were very poor and we lived in a remote village. One day, on the road, I found the broken pieces of a mirror. A German motorcycle had been wrecked in that place.
>
> I tried to find all the pieces and put them together, but it was not possible, so I kept only the largest piece. This one. And by scratching it on a stone, I made it round. I began to play with it as a toy and became fascinated by the fact that I could reflect light into dark places where the sun would never shine. . . . I kept the little mirror, and as I went about my growing up, I would take it out in idle moments. . . . As I became a man, I grew to understand that this was not just a child's game but a metaphor for what I might do with my life. I came to understand that I am not the light or the source of light. But light—truth, understanding, knowledge—is there, and it will only shine in many dark places if I reflect it.[15]

The professor in this story found meaning in reflecting light into the dark places of human hearts. Maybe this could be the meaning of your life, too: reflecting the light of Jesus Christ into the dark places of the world and the dark places of the human heart. Although the light doesn't belong to you and doesn't originate with you, it is yours to reflect and share.

Jesus said, "I am the light of the world. If you follow me, you won't have to walk in darkness, because you will have the light that leads to life" (John 8:12 NLT).

If you choose to reflect the light of Jesus Christ into the dark places, in the many ways that are possible for you to do, and if you let that choice become the one compelling reason for your whole life, the reason you get up in the morning and go about whatever you do, then you just might discover what it means to live, really live, and never have to ask, "What is the meaning of life?"

* * *

Norman Neaves, an Oklahoma City pastor, tells the story of a young couple who made an appointment with their pastor to discuss their upcoming wedding. At least, the pastor thought that was why they made the appointment; but as it turned out, that was not the reason at all.

Arriving at the appointed time, the young man said, "As you know, we're getting married soon and you're going to be doing our wedding. But the reason we're here today is because we want to talk about joining the church. Neither one of us has ever been baptized."

The young man added, "We think it's important that we put Christ at the center of our lives right now, before we get married, because we believe we can have a wonderful life together—if we build our lives on belief in Christ."

And so, a Sunday or two later, this engaged couple stood before the congregation to profess their faith in Christ and to be baptized into the Christian faith. A few months after that, they stood before the congregation again to be joined together as husband and wife and to go forward into their future as a new couple in Christ.

That young couple won't have a perfect life together, for none of us do. They will face hardships, disappointments, and tragedies, like the rest of us; and they will encounter joys, thrills, and successes as well. However, I believe they will be able to handle the storms of life a whole lot better than most, because they have something beneath them that's strong and solid. After all, there will be three people in their relationship: the young man, the young woman, and the Lord.

I wish everyone had that relationship. But how will the young people in your community ever come to believe in Jesus and place him at the center of their relationships unless someone witnesses to them and invites them to be part of the Lord's church?

That witness might come from a friend, a relative, a co-worker, or a stranger. It might even come from you.

While attending a Billy Graham Association training event, I learned that the typical new convert had experienced twenty-four witnesses or invitations before they finally said yes to the Lord. Those witnesses might have been in the context of an hour-long discussion or even the briefest of encounters.

The number twenty-four is probably about right for my own spiritual journey. I grew up in the church, but my "twenty-fourth" moment happened with the simplest of gestures some forty years ago. I was a sophomore in high school and at a real crossroads in my life.

One Friday evening, with much encouragement from my parents, I decided to attend a weekend of special events at our church. As soon as I arrived, I began to feel self-conscious and out of place. I didn't see anyone I knew and decided to leave. So I called my parents to pick me up and walked toward the door to the parking lot.

But you know what happened at that very moment? Chris, the youth minister, called out my name and motioned me over to his office. That weekend, through his attention, my life was changed, and it has never been quite the same since.

What if Chris had not called out my name? What if he had not taken a special interest in me? What if he had not singled me out of that crowd? What if that simple moment had never taken place at all?

I'll tell you what if: I'd likely not be here now. I'd likely not have experienced the wonderful life I've found in Christ. I'd likely not have worked as a summer youth minister myself. I'd likely not have met a young woman named Marcia. My sons Charles and David likely never would have been born, and Marlie, Grayson, Owen, and Blake would be someone else's grandchildren.

My life with Christ, and my daily life since, was changed because one man took the time to single me out at precisely the moment when I was walking out of the church. If he hadn't done it, I am convinced that my life would have gone in an entirely different direction.

Some of you no doubt will say, "I could never witness. I don't know enough about the Bible." Others may be thinking, "Well, I guess I could go on a mission trip. I could travel to Mexico or Haiti or Belize to witness. But I sure would have to save up. A trip like that would probably cost a lot of money." But thankfully, you don't have to study the Bible for twenty years to witness. Nor do you need to travel to Mexico or Haiti to witness.

Jesus had a plan. Listen to these words of Jesus when he sent his twelve disciples out to witness.

> "Don't begin by traveling to some far-off place to convert unbelievers. And don't try to be dramatic by tackling some public enemy. Go to the lost, confused people right here in the neighborhood. Tell them that the kingdom is here. Bring health to the sick. Raise the dead. Touch the untouchables. Kick out the demons. You have been treated generously, so live generously. Don't think you have to put on a fundraising campaign before you start. You don't need a lot of equipment. You are the equipment, and all you need to keep that going is three meals a day." (Matthew 10:5-10 *THE MESSAGE*)

*   *   *

I believe there are people within your circle of influence who will never come to faith in Christ unless you witness to them. There are family members, friends at school, neighbors, people you work with, and people you do business with who will never come to faith in Christ unless you witness to them.

You and I are surrounded by people who have no faith involvement. The American Church Research Project (www.theamerican church.org) reports that on a typical Sunday in the United States, only 17% of the population is in worship. If this research is correct, it means that on a typical Sunday in the United States, 50 million people are in worship and 260 million are not.[16]

Do those numbers bother you? Are you concerned that perhaps 260 million of your neighbors stayed home last Sunday? Does your heart break for them? Do you long for them to discover what you have experienced in worshiping the Lord? Do you long for them to receive forgiveness for their sins? Do you long for them to make strong Christian friendships like you have made? Do you long for them to find salvation and the eternal hope of heaven?

That same research group has found that worship attendance patterns are not consistent in every county across the country. Worship is lower than average in some counties and higher than average in others.

If you are in one of those rare counties where worship attendance approaches 40%, does it concern you that 60% of your neighbors choose to not attend worship? If you are in the typical county, does it concern you that 83% of your neighbors choose not to?

This week I want to invite you and challenge you to add these neighbors to your prayer list. Pray that these "lost sheep" might be saved. Pray that these "prodigal" daughters and sons might come to their senses and turn their hearts toward their heavenly home. Pray until every church in your neighborhood is full every Sunday.

It has been my habit on Sunday afternoons to make a brief doorstep visit to the home of each first-time worship guest. I've knocked on hundreds of doors early on Sunday afternoons. On many occasions it has been the home of a young couple with early elementary-age children. Frequently, since they have young children, one of the spouses has been anxious for the family to find a church home and the other spouse has resisted. Typically this Sunday is the first time the reluctant spouse has finally given in and said, "Okay, I'll try it one time."

When families such as this step though our church doors for the first time, they will be deciding whether they will ever attend a second time. During that first time in worship, if we fail to welcome them warmly, if we scare them by welcoming them too enthusiastically, if our nursery doesn't meet their standards for safe care, if the music is poorly performed, if the sermon is disjointed, if the bathrooms are dirty, or if we fail in some other way to meet their high expectations, they will not return. After worship, on the way to the car, the reluctant spouse will say, "Never again. I gave in and tried it once. But you're not going to get me back in that place again."

Decide today that you will do your part to offer excellence to worship guests, so the guests will say, "That wasn't so bad. Would you mind if we came back again next Sunday?"

* * *

Dr. Mordecai Johnson, formerly president of Howard University and a contemporary of Dr. Martin Luther King, told a story of growing up in a small southern town.

He reported that an evangelist came to that town for a revival, and a small boy was drawn to the big tent. Each night, the young child sat in one of the chairs that was reserved for children in the back of the tent.

As the meetings came to a close at the end of the week, it was announced that the climax would be on Sunday morning, when all those who were ready to receive Christ would be baptized. Those who wanted to be baptized were to arrive on Sunday dressed in white clothes.

The child hurried home and told his mother what he wanted to do. At his request, his mother took a sheet off one of the beds and fashioned him a little white robe.

Proudly, happily, and somewhat frightened, the child made his way to the tent that Sunday. Oh, there was a crowd! There was singing and praying! The ushers looked over the crowd, and when they saw someone dressed in white, that person was led to the altar and baptized into the church of Jesus Christ.

Late that night, after the revival service was over, the crowd dispersed—all except one, a little child dressed in a white robe who stood alone, still waiting, because no usher had noticed him, talked to him, or led him to the altar, and no preacher had baptized him.

I propose to you that that small boy is still standing there, in a hundred front yards and living rooms in your neighborhood. Could it be that there are 50 children, 500 children, or 5,000 children who are not in any church today?

How many children and youth in your community have never walked through the doors of a church? How many have never been invited to attend vacation Bible school, Sunday school, youth fellowship, or church camp? How many have never been baptized?

How many of these young people are making life-changing decisions about what kind of adult they will be, what kind of parent they will be, and what kind of citizen they will be? How many are making these decisions without the influence of the church, the wisdom of a Sunday school teacher, the support of Christian aunts and uncles or friends like you, and without the power of the Holy Spirit in their lives?

Decide today that your church will be an inviting church—that you will discover the joy of inviting, not just on special occasions but as part of your daily routine. Decide today that you will look for opportunities to invite friends, neighbors, work associates, recreational associates, and neighbors to attend church with you.

Decide today to explore new ways to invite unchurched residents to worship with you. Decide today to reach the children and youth in your community for Jesus' sake, for heaven's sake. Decide today to continue this mission until every "lost sheep" has been found, and every "prodigal" daughter and son has come to their senses and turned their hearts toward their heavenly home.

Lord, I lift up to you the members of my extended family who are not close to you. I also lift up to you some of my friends, co-workers, and classmates who have not yet welcomed you into their lives. I confess that I don't have all the answers and sometimes feel awkward bringing up the subject of religion. And yet, Lord, my heart breaks when I think of those close to me who have never experienced the forgiveness of sin, the joy of your salvation, the blessing of Christian friendships, and the hope of eternity. Lord, use me. Help me to know what I might do or say to present the Christian faith in a winsome way. Amen.

AN INVITATION

Bob Pierson

The experience of coming to know Christ can often be through a simple invitation. In John 1:40-46 we have two stories: Andrew inviting Peter to meet Jesus, and then Philip inviting Nathaniel. These stories sometimes seem so basic, but frequently the faith is transmitted in this simple way.

Doug was going through a difficult time. He and his wife were divorced, and the children were teenagers. There was a lot of chaos in his life. He was not a committed Christian, nor was he involved in the church. He was searching.

Doug's fifteen-year-old son, Adam, was invited by one of his friends to a concert at a church. Adam visited the church, met other teenagers, and eventually stayed. Over time he became deeply committed to Christ. Next Adam invited his twelve-year-old sister, and she was touched by the invitation. She went and became involved in the youth group. Soon after she made a commitment to Christ. The two children then invited their mother. In the midst of her struggle with divorce, she too committed her life to Christ and became involved in the church.

Doug, still distant from God, was the next target of their efforts. One night they invited Doug to a concert in which Adam was involved. Doug was touched by the experience, started attending the church, and later became involved himself. Out of that experience, Doug grew deeply in the Christian faith, matured in leadership, and became chairman of the evangelism committee. The excitement of following Christ came in stages for Doug. He is now deeply committed to Christ and leading the church in evangelism. He has just written a new book entitled *Reach*, which describes how social media can help the church reach more people for Christ.

Bob Pierson is founder and Executive Director of Leadership Nexus. He served as senior pastor of Christ Church in Tulsa, Oklahoma, for 37 years, increasing attendance from 200 to over 1600. Leadership Nexus exists to help the church be more effective in proclaiming the Gospel to the world.

5.
FINANCIAL GIVING

A pastor was concerned that his church never seemed to have enough money. The church was always late in paying the Sunday school literature bill. They cut back on air conditioning and heating to lower the utility bill. They withheld money that would have supported foreign missions. Finally it dawned on the pastor what the problem was.

Every time new believers came forward for baptism, they would go to a side room to change clothes before stepping into the baptistry pool to be immersed. It dawned on the pastor that they always left their purses or billfolds in the changing room.

"In my church," the pastor concluded, "I have baptized their hearts, but their pocketbooks remain powder dry."

I'm afraid that is true in most of our churches. When we baptize, we just don't use enough water to reach dad's back pocket or mom's purse.

As Christians, most of us have stood before a congregation to profess our faith. Most of us responded positively to a question such as

"Will you support the church with your prayers, presence, gifts, service, and witness?"

Most of us attended some form of membership class or had a conversation with the pastor in which we learned that church membership involved:

- a decision to be a committed follower and disciple of Jesus Christ
- praying for the pastor, church officers, teachers, and those whose health or hearts are broken
- reading and meditating on the Bible daily
- being present in worship every week that we are physically able
- sharing the good news of Jesus Christ with others in a winsome way and inviting them to join us in worship and on the journey toward a commitment to Christ
- supporting the church financially with a ten percent tithe, the biblical standard
- serving the Lord by offering our time, the sweat of our brow, and the blisters on our hands

We also came to understand from those conversations that we were not to "pick one" of these to do but rather to "pick them all" and to keep them faithfully.

*   *   *

For some of you, financial giving is the most difficult of these holy habits, and you're not alone. When Christian theologian and Methodism founder, John Wesley, was a college student at Oxford, a custodian knocked on his door one cold night as he was studying. Wesley answered and they talked briefly. As the custodian was leaving, Wesley noticed that the man had on a thin jacket and remarked, "You ought to put on a heavier coat." The custodian responded, "This is the only coat I have, and I thank God for this coat."

When Wesley realized the man did not have enough money to buy warm clothes, he asked if he had enough to buy food. The custodian's reply was essentially the same: "I have had nothing today but water to drink, but I thank God for the water."

Wesley was getting uncomfortable with the conversation and said something about it being time for the man to get home and crawl into a warm bed. And the custodian responded, "I thank God I have a dry floor to sleep on tonight."

Deeply moved by the man's simple faith in God, Wesley asked, "You thank God when you have nothing to wear, nothing to eat, and no warm bed upon which to lie. What else do you thank God for?"

The custodian replied, "I thank God that he has given me the gift of life, a heart to love him, and a deep desire to serve him. What more could a man ever want?"[17]

John Wesley was so moved by the custodian's words that he wrote in his journal that night, "I shall never forget that man. He convinced me that there's something in religion to which I am a stranger."

This encounter led Wesley to develop a strong opinion about money. Later he wrote: "Make all you can. Save all you can. Give all you can."[18] And he did just that. Wesley gave everything away. Upon his death, there was hardly any estate at all. He lived modestly so that he could give toward building new churches, purchasing religious books for class meetings, and supporting ministries to widows, orphans, and prisoners.

*   *   *

I remember very well when my parents began to give sacrificially. They were about forty years old, and I was in elementary school. My family was active at St. Matthew's United Methodist Church in Houston, Texas, and the church began a ten-year emphasis on giving. The invitation was rather simple: "If you do not currently support the church financially, begin this year giving 2% of your income to the church. If you are currently giving 5% of your income, begin this year increasing your gift just one step to 6%. Wherever you are in your giving, grow just one step each year until you have reached that biblical standard of the tithe, 10%."

If I remember correctly, my parents were giving about 4% at the time. That year, our family made a commitment that we would grow one step each year, and we did.

I say "we" because that decision to make the tithe a priority affected the whole family. With my parents giving more money to the church, there was less disposable income for the minor luxuries my brother and I previously enjoyed. Also, my brother and I began to tithe our allowance and any money we earned by mowing lawns for neighbors.

This pattern of tithing was in place when Marcia and I married. It seemed natural to follow in the footsteps of our parents. When we had a household income of $500 a month, we would give $50 a month to the church. And we have continued to give at least 10% to the church.

I understand, of course, that for some people tithing does not seem natural. The idea of placing any money in the offering plate is a very difficult thought.

Most of us struggle with the desire for more. We want more money and the things that money can buy. We want bigger houses, nicer cars, more clothes, and longer vacations. We want more of everything. This desire for more is fed by our economy and by the marketing that drives it. When we turn on the morning news, listen to the radio driving to the office, or access the Internet, we are bombarded with a parade of commercials that offer happiness. We become convinced that if we just had the particular item being advertised at the moment, then we would be happy. We become convinced that more is better and that we need all these things.

Society calls this "materialism." The Bible calls it "greed."

In their book *Money Drunk/Money Sober: 90 Days to Financial Freedom*, Julia Cameron and Mark Bryan propose that people can become addicted to money and that this addiction can be very destructive. They describe several people. Do you know anyone like them?

Do you know anyone like Pamela? Pamela steals from her husband's wallet. She likes to go shopping but hides her purchases. She lies to her husband about where her money goes. She invents household emergencies, such as appliance and car repairs that never happened. She borrows from her children's birthday money. She returns groceries to the store to get the cash. Pamela is addicted to money, and it is affecting her marriage. Do you know anyone like Pamela?

Do you know anyone like Daniel? Daniel is afraid to answer the phone. Far too often, it is someone calling about an overdue bill. Daniel sees something on television or in a catalog, and he wants it. He wants it desperately and he buys it. His credit cards are all at the limit or beyond. He struggles to pay even a portion of the minimum due each month. He has borrowed money from all his friends. He intends to pay it back but never has the money to. His wife doesn't understand why they never have any money. And Daniel is afraid to answer the phone, afraid to go to the grocery store, afraid he will run into someone he owes money to. Daniel is addicted to money. Daniel seems unable to live within his means. Do you know anyone like Daniel?[19]

For these people, money has taken control of their lives. They are addicted to money. Money has become the number-one priority in life.

The first thing they need to do is to tear up those credit cards today.

The second is to begin to live within their means, cutting back on housing, transportation, and clothing costs.

Their love of money is putting their marriages at risk and affecting their employment and future. They are driven to spend more than they have. This drive is robbing them of the joys in life and certainly robbing them of the joy of giving back to God.

Pastors have problems with this too. A few years ago, a bishop was traveling to each district to meet the pastors. I remember sitting in a circle of chairs—about fifty of us meeting with our new bishop.

In response to a question about pastors' salaries, the bishop said, "If you are finding your self-worth in the amount of money you are paid, you'd better find a different job. I suggest that you find your self-worth while you kneel in prayer, and in the lives you touch, the hearts that are changed, and the souls that are saved. If you find you still don't have enough money to buy all the things that you want, I know an answer: Turn your wanter down. Just reach out, grab the dial, and turn your wanter down. Keep turning it down until you do have enough money for all your needs and wants."

I thought at the time that the bishop was speaking only to me. But I was not the only pastor who listened that day.

I was visiting the office of one of our young pastors. She said, "The problem is this: My husband and I want to give to the church but never seem to have any money after we pay the bills. So we went to a financial counselor last month. The counselor said that the only way we could give any money to the church was to 'cut the fat.'"

Now, I know this young pastor. I know the kind of the car she drives. I know the kind of clothes she wears. I know the exact amount of her income. So, when she said "cut the fat," I could not imagine how she could live more simply.

But here's what she said next: "When we got home that night after seeing the financial counselor, we decided that we would 'cut the fat.' We like to go out to eat, and since we don't have children yet, we go out to eat almost every evening after work. That night, we made a list of the fourteen restaurants we like and took twelve off our list, leaving the two least expensive ones. We decided we cannot spend any more than that. We also canceled our cable television. We will just watch the broadcast channels."

But she wasn't finished. She went on to say: "I love to shop for clothes, but I decided I won't buy any more clothes this year or next. We've done all this so we can give $32 to the church each Sunday."

Earlier in this chapter, I wrote that for some of us, the holy habit of financial generosity may be the most difficult of the six steps in our commitment to Christ. I think it was difficult back in Jesus' day, too. Perhaps that is why Jesus talked more about money and how to use it than he spoke about prayer, heaven, or hell. He told forty-three parables that are recorded in the New Testament, and twenty-seven of them are about money and possessions. United Methodist pastor Herb Miller has counted 500 verses in the Bible on prayer, 500 on faith, and more than 2,000 on money and what money buys.[20]

Jesus talked a lot about money, and I'm confident that the synagogue offering increased in every town where he taught.

* * *

Today I invite you to decide what you will give the church. I invite you to make a commitment to grow one step. Dig out your tax papers. Find the percentage you gave last year. Commit to stepping up the percentage each year going forward, until you have reached the biblical standard of the tithe, 10%.

I invite you to step up to tithing. You will be blessed!

I offer you this invitation from personal experience. I had a life-changing moment my first summer as a youth minister. Brother

I. L. Claude was a saintly retired pastor in our church. In his youth, he rode horseback to the circuit of churches that he served. Many times he rode across a river, then built a fire on the other side to dry his clothes. He slept many a night under the stars.

Brother Claude knew I was going to Hendrix College and that I was in training to be a pastor. While we were standing in his front yard one day, he offered me one bit of advice on which to build my ministry. He invited me to decide, at the tender age of nineteen, who was Lord of my life and to manage my money accordingly. It was one of those life-changing "God moments."

Brother I. L. Claude put it this way: "Give the first 10% of your paycheck back to God. The second 10% of your paycheck is for savings and investing toward retirement. Then live on the 80% that remains."

"I've done that all my life," said Brother Claude. He turned and motioned toward his home. "I have been faithful to God, and God has been faithful to me."

My income at the time was $75 a week. Brother Claude invited me to put $7.50 in the offering, $7.50 in savings, and live on the remaining $60.

For more than thirty years, my wife and I have strived to be faithful to those guidelines. What a great joy! The money we have kept to pay bills has disappeared. But the money we gave to the church is still enriching the lives of children and youth, supporting our missionaries overseas, and working for the Lord.

Today, consider the invitation to step up to tithing. Consider giving 4% this year, 6% next year, 8% the following year, and finally 10%.

As you ponder the invitation, reflect on these words from 1 Timothy, chapter six (GNT):

> You must teach and preach these things. Whoever teaches a different doctrine and does not agree with the true words of our Lord Jesus Christ and with the teaching of our religion is swollen with pride and knows nothing (verse 3).

> Well, religion does make us very rich, if we are satisfied with what we have. What did we bring into the world? Nothing! What can we take out of the world? Nothing! So then, if we have food and clothes,

that should be enough for us. But those who want to get rich fall into temptation and are caught in the trap of many foolish and harmful desires, which pull them down to ruin and destruction. For the love of money is a source of all kinds of evil. Some have been so eager to have it that they have wandered away from the faith and have broken their hearts with many sorrows (verses 6-11a).

Command those who are rich in the things of this life not to be proud, but to place their hope, not in such an uncertain thing as riches, but in God, who generously gives us everything for our enjoyment. Command them to do good, to be rich in good works, to be generous and ready to share with others. In this way they will store up for themselves a treasure which will be a solid foundation for the future. And then they will be able to win the life which is true life (verses 17-19).

O Lord, once again we are faced with priorities. What do we want the most? Do we want to be rich on earth or rich in heaven? Do we want to be generous? Do we want to return to you, O Lord, a portion of our resources? Lord, help us to know what we should do in response to this invitation. In Jesus' name we pray. Amen.

You Tithe But . . .

J. Clif Christopher

The other day I was visiting with a young man who told me about his father, who lived in a city not too far away. He said that his dad faithfully sent a check for child support and would buy birthday and Christmas presents, but rarely expressed a desire to be with him. As the young man spoke, I could see the pain in his eyes and on his face. He said that even in the summer when he went to see his father, the father was often busy and would send him off to a cousin or family friend. It was great to get the money and gifts, but more than anything the young man wanted love. He wanted a relationship that his father obviously could not or would not provide.

Not long after that, I found myself talking with a woman who was angry with her ex-husband, who, though he talked on the phone with their child and visited him, would not pay child support or purchase school supplies. The woman said, "He thinks withholding money is just hurting me and not his son, but it is hurting his son. I can't buy my son all the things he needs to wear to school and to dress properly. The attention is nice, but it is hollow without money to back it up."

All of this got me thinking about how I feel about tithing. I have been a long-time tither, giving God at least ten percent of my earnings, and on occasion I have lapsed into thinking that now that I have tithed, I can do exactly as I please. On the other hand, some may want to "trade" tithing for giving their time, assuming that God has some sort of point system, and they can gain enough points in one area to make up for another.

I found myself remembering Matthew 23:23, where Jesus said (to paraphrase), "You tithe but . . . " Jesus was not saying that giving the tithe was bad, not at all. He was saying that only giving the tithe and not loving God or loving our neighbor misses the point. In other words, it's not our money that Jesus is after but a relationship. God wants us to be in a loving relationship with him more than anything else, and tithing is and should be one part of that expression of love. I should want to tithe, but not so I will get something in return. I should want to at least tithe because of the simple fact that I love God and I'm so grateful for all he has done for me.

A father who says he wants to have a relationship with a child but refuses to share a portion of his wealth with him or her is not a father who truly loves his child. And a father who only sends his child money, no matter how much, but does not desire to spend time with him, is not a father who truly loves his child. Both cases reveal a person who is too much in love with himself or herself, a person who values money or time more than a loving relationship.

Tithing is important to me, but not to gain points or go to heaven; it is important in order to have and sustain the kind of loving relationship with my heavenly Father that is necessary for me to live.

J. Clif Christopher founded the Horizons Stewardship Company in 1992 following twenty years in pastoral ministry. He has led consultations in over 400 churches, conferences, synods, and dioceses in all phases of building, finance, and church growth. He is the author of Not Your Parents' Offering Plate *and* Whose Offering Plate Is It?

6.
HANDS-ON SERVICE IN JESUS' NAME

What do you want to do with your life? What imprint do you want to leave on this earth? Do you want to be known as a spiritual giant, a great person of prayer, as a person of compassion, or a sacrificial servant of the Lord?

I suppose you could pretend, building up a false front. That might be easier than being genuine. The problem is that you would know it was a lie.

What do you want to do with your life?

In his book *At the End of the Day*, James Moore tells the story of Orville Kelly. Orville went for a physical exam at the age of forty-three and was diagnosed with cancer. This was an especially difficult cancer, the kind that doesn't respond to radiation, surgery, or chemotherapy. Orville was told, "You have six months, maybe thirty-six months at most, but no more."

As the news spread about Orville's diagnosis, friends didn't know what to say, so they avoided Orville. His wife, Wanda, didn't want to talk about it. "Just don't think about it," she would often say to Orville. Their children weren't even told.

One day, Orville said, "Wanda, we have got to talk. I'm not dead yet. Yes, I've got cancer, and yes, I'll probably die from it. But I'm not dead yet, and we've just got to talk." So they did —honestly, openly, and lovingly. Then Orville said, "Let's have a big barbecue, invite all our friends over, and start living again. I don't want to waste any more time."

A few weeks after the barbecue, Orville told his wife, "I'm not going to get up in the morning anymore thinking, 'This is one day less to live.' Rather, I'm going to take on a new attitude. I'm going to thank God, every day, for the gift of that day." Orville decided to form a club called MTC—Make Today Count.

"After all," he said, "everyone is terminal. I simply know that my terminus has been more clearly determined. None of us know for sure when we are going to die. So, I am going to make every day count for something wonderful. I'm going to see every day as a special and gracious gift from God."[21]

In Psalm 118:24, we read: "This is the day that the Lord made; let us rejoice and be glad in it." How are you going to spend your days? Are you making every day count, or is life passing you by?

1 Corinthians 12 introduces an idea that just might change your life:

> And now, dear brothers and sisters, I will write about the special abilities the Holy Spirit gives to each of us, for I must correct your misunderstandings about them. . . . Now there are different kinds of spiritual gifts, but it is the same Holy Spirit who is the source of them all. There are different kinds of service in the church, but it is the same Lord we are serving. There are different ways God works in our lives, but it is the same God who does the work through all of us. A spiritual gift is given to each of us as a means of helping the entire church. (NLT)

The point is this: As Christians we each have a mission to accomplish in Jesus' name. The Spirit of God has given each of us the gifts we need to accomplish our particular role in his church.

I like the way my friend John said it to me one Sunday: "I can't sing. I can't teach. I can't speak in public. But I can sweat. If you ever need work done, I'm your man."

John has more talents than he recognizes and uses them behind the scenes all the time. For example, he initiated and sponsored a church-wide barbecue to raise money to retire the church's debt on our new fellowship hall. For a month he sold tickets in the lobby. He tapped a dozen folks on the shoulder to help cook and serve the dinner. He recruited another dozen to help set up the room for the dinner and to clean up afterward.

Like John, you have talents and abilities. If you have the talent of singing, why aren't you in the choir? If you have the gift of loving children, why aren't you serving in the children's ministry?

What are your God-given talents and abilities? Are you using them to serve the Lord?

*   *   *

When you take the step of serving in Jesus' name, I wonder where you will serve. I wonder where you will "get blisters" in Jesus' name. I don't know the answer. What I do know is that the Lord will take this journey of service with you and will guide you to wonderful places where you can make a difference by the sweat of your brow and the strength of your hands.

Maybe you'll be like Mrs. Harrison. She was about sixty years old. Although her own children had grown up, married, and moved out of state, God had given her a special love for teenagers. So, Mrs. Harrison was at church every Sunday night. She made sure the youth group ran smoothly. She coordinated parents to bring snack suppers. She had a Wednesday morning prayer breakfast for the youth before school. On those mornings, she brought doughnuts, orange juice, and milk, and she opened the sanctuary for the youth to kneel in prayer before breakfast. She did this for years and years without fail. She was like a second grandmother to the youth.

Has it ever dawned on you that *you* could be a Mrs. Harrison at your church?

Let me tell you about Mr. Edwards. He worked for the phone company. He was on the road a great deal, but that didn't keep him from serving the Lord at church. Mr. Edwards was a parent with two sons in the youth group. He not only loved his boys but he had enough patience and love for all the youth in the church, including me. Every Sunday night he would pick out three or four of us to do the program for the next Sunday. He met with us midweek and helped us put the Sunday evening program together, including skits, Scripture reading, or maybe a video clip to watch. He also taught the youth Sunday school class. He was like a second father to our youth group. Has it ever dawned on you that *you* could be a Mr. Edwards at your church?

Let me tell you about Mr. Keller. He was president of the bank downtown and had a big house in a new subdivision. He also had a special place in his heart for the youth at church, and those of us in the youth group knew it. Whether it was a Friday night discussion group or a Monday evening prayer meeting, his home was always available. At work, his office door was always open to us. Every time I walked into the bank, he would walk over to me at the teller counter and speak with me. I had less than twenty dollars in the bank, but he wanted to invest his time in my life. Did any of the youth need a summer job? He would help. Did we have problems at home? He would listen. Did anyone need an adult to talk to? His door was open. Has it ever dawned on you that *you* could be a Mr. Keller at your church?

Then there's Marcia. She was a college student—too old for the youth group. But she gave her time to the youth ministry all summer. Youth trip? She would be a driver. Youth swim party? She was in the pool. Prayer vigil? She brought Cokes. She was like a big sister to the youth. Has it ever dawned on you that *you* could be a Marcia at your church?

Of course, there are other ministries at church besides youth. Let me tell you about Fran. She was in her mid-seventies and had more than her share of health problems. However, she was at church every Sunday, standing by the door before worship and shaking every hand, saying, "I'm so glad you are here today." Fran was at the door after worship, too. "Thank you for coming today," she would say. "I hope to see you next Sunday." On Mondays, she sent handwritten notes to worship guests the first seven times they visited. On Tuesdays she sent handwritten notes to any members who had missed three or more Sundays. On Wednesdays, as a volunteer at the local hospital, she would stop by to visit any patients related to the church. Has it ever dawned on you that *you* could be a Fran at your church?

What do you want to be? What do you want do? You can do it in Christ's name by serving.

*   *   *

A few years ago Chris moved to a new town to start a small business. His family joined the church I was serving. He had to travel a great deal, and the airline tickets were expensive. But Chris's business has grown since then. He now has secretaries and a hallway full of executives in his company. He still flies three or four times a week, but never in coach, always first class.

On one of his East Coast trips, Chris was waiting to board the plane. At the gate, he noticed several dozen soldiers. As an army veteran of Desert Storm, he went over to visit with the soldiers. They were headed home after serving in Iraq. One of the soldiers was distressed. He had been bumped by the airline. The flight was oversold. The young soldier said, "My wife has already left the house for the airport to pick me up. She thinks I'm going to be there. She's brought our three kids and the baby I've never seen who was born just three months ago."

Chris walked over to the gate ticket agent and asked, "Are there any seats left on this plane?" The agent turned to the screen for a moment and answered, "Just one. It's in first class." Chris said, "I want to buy that ticket for the soldier sitting over there. Here is my account number."

Later, as Chris and the soldier sat next to each other during the flight, the soldier said, "Mister, I was sitting at the gate praying to God, asking for some way to get home to see my family. And God sent you to me."

What do you think? Was the businessman foolish? Did the Lord use Chris to answer the veteran's prayer? Has God ever called on you to be the answer to someone's prayer? Did you respond?

Maybe you have a particular passion to follow James 1:27: "Pure and lasting religion in the sight of God our father means that we must care for widows and fatherless children in their troubles, and refuse to let the world corrupt us."

Joe has that kind of passion. Joe discovered that the Angel Tree program in his community did not serve any of the foster children. Joe, through his church, adopted that mission. Beginning that year, his church provided Angel Tree gifts for all ninety of the foster children in the county. Has it ever dawned on you that you could be a Joe in your community?

Patricia and Tammy, registered nurses, discovered that about three newborn babies every week went home from the local hospital dressed only in a T-shirt. It bothered Patricia and Tammy that those babies did not have a blanket and layette for their first trip home. Working through their church, they adopted that mission. Beginning the following Sunday, the nurses in the maternity ward were given a small stockpile of new layette sets. On the first Sunday of every month, the congregation was invited to bring layettes and place them in a basket that was prominently displayed in the lobby. Through Patricia and Tammy, for more than a decade the church has made sure that even the poorest mothers have had a new set of clothes and a blanket when it's time to take their new babies home. Has it ever dawned on you that you could be the Patricia or Tammy in your church?

Maybe you have a particular passion for Matthew 25:37-39 (NLT):

> Then these righteous ones will reply, "Lord, when did we ever see you hungry and feed you? Or thirsty and give you something to drink? Or a stranger and show you hospitality? Or naked and give you clothing? When did we ever see you sick or in prison and visit you?" And the King will say, "I tell you the truth, when you did it to one of the least of these my brothers and sisters, you were doing it to me!"

Allen had compassion for the elderly poor. He began putting week-long mission trips together, during which the youth would work in the summer heat to build wheelchair ramps, paint houses, and make minor repairs in some of the poorest counties in the Ozarks. Today, twenty-five years later, Ozark Mission Project has provided life-changing, hands-on mission and ministry opportunities for 15,000 middle school, high school, and college-age students. Since 1986, young people have been venturing out of their comfort zone to all areas of the Ozarks to experience a unique way to practice our call to serve those in need, by offering assistance to 5,500 elderly and disadvantaged people who need home repairs and Christian hospitality that includes visitation, food, devotions, and prayer. Has it ever dawned on you that you could be the Allen in your church?

Jack had a problem with drinking and partying. Too often, Jack would leave his wife and children at home to go to an all-night party. His lifestyle and choices robbed the family of any financial security and deprived the children of any stability at home. One morning, after a night of parties and drinking, Jack woke up and realized it was Christmas. He also realized he had no presents for the children. Jack called the owner of the local drugstore and asked if the store was open. The owner said, "Jack, this is Christmas morning. The store is closed for the day. I need to be at home with my own children."

Jack begged, "Please, please, I don't have any presents for my children!" The owner finally gave in and agreed to meet Jack at the store. As the owner unlocked the door, he realized that Jack had very little money. So, out of love for the children, the owner said, "Jack, this is Christmas. Everything is free. Pick out whatever your children need."

Jack, almost in tears, was deeply touched by the words. Later that day, after the children had opened their presents, Jack and his wife sat at the kitchen table. For the first time in their married life, Jack and his wife prayed together, and Jack accepted Jesus Christ as his Lord and Savior.

A few months later, out of the newly discovered love Jack had found, he began thinking about other men in his town who had lost their way, their focus, their sobriety, and in some cases their families. Jack started the Gospel Rescue Mission, first in his hometown of Fort Smith, Arkansas, and later in nearby Van Buren. The mission is still there. For forty years, volunteers have been offering help, and they have been offering Jesus. Has it ever dawned on you that you could be Jack to your church and community? Has it ever dawned on you that you could be like the storeowner in Jack's community?

Bob was concerned about the children in the neighborhood where his church was located. With their parents commuting from the city thirty-five miles to the south, many of the children were home alone after school until six or seven o'clock in the evening. During the summer, the children were poorly supervised all day while parents were at work. The church did not have the financial resources or the volunteers to provide the five-day-a-week program that was needed. But Bob, working through the church council and the local United Way agency, arranged for the Boys and Girls Club to open a ministry in the church fellowship hall. As a result of this combined effort, one hundred and fifty children find a safe and enriching environment at the church every day after school and all day during the summer. Has it ever dawned on you that you could be the Bob in your church?

Mrs. Cooper was concerned that her church did not have a nursery. She noticed that when young families visited the church, they were disappointed that the church could offer no care for their young ones during worship. Mrs. Cooper was in her mid-seventies, yet her love for the church and for children compelled her to provide nursery equipment at the church. Every Sunday, she would stand at the door to greet worship guests. If a young family visited, she would offer to take care of their little ones during worship. Has it ever dawned on you that you could be a Mrs. Cooper and volunteer in your church's nursery?

*   *   *

Today, we invite you to increase the time you serve in Jesus' name. Consider giving an hour a week, or perhaps three hours a week, to be a servant. Perhaps the Lord is calling you to full-time Christian ministry.

As you consider this invitation, reflect on the following words of Scripture:

> Work hard and do not be lazy. Serve the Lord with a heart full of devotion. Let your hope keep you joyful, be patient in your troubles, and pray at all times. (Romans 12:11-12 GNT)

> And all of you must put on the apron of humility, to serve one another; for the scripture says, "God resists the proud, but shows favor to the humble." Humble yourselves, then, under God's mighty hand, so that he will lift you up in his own good time. Leave all your worries with him, because he cares for you. (1 Peter 5:5-7)

> Instead, let love make you serve one another. For the whole Law is summed up in one commandment: "Love your neighbor as you love yourself." (Galatians 5:14-16 GNT)

And when you serve Christ in this way, you please God and are approved by others. So then, we must always aim at those things that bring peace and that help strengthen one another. (Romans 14:18-19 GNT)

Lord, could you use someone like me? Do I have any talents or abilities that might be used in your service? Could you use the hours of my day and the strength of my hands to further your kingdom? If there are ways I might serve you, help me to discern them and give me the courage to say, "Yes, Lord, here I am." Lord, help me to know what I should do with this invitation to serve. In Jesus' name I pray. Amen.

A MAN NAMED ERNIE

Minerva G. Carcaño

Early one Saturday morning I found myself on my knees in the dirt, next to a row of young people. Together we were planting flowers around the small, simple home of a man whom these young people helped to emerge from poverty. They had met the man at a homeless shelter, given him a sandwich, and prayed for him. When they left him behind at that homeless shelter, it had disturbed their spirits.

"How can we just walk away and leave this man homeless?" they asked themselves.

Ernie was his name. His struggle and his spirit so moved these young people that they couldn't forget him. They started taking Ernie to church with them on Sundays. They convinced their parents to help them lift Ernie out of his poverty. Ernie, however, didn't want to be patronized; he'd had enough of that in his life. The young people knew they didn't want to do anything that would hurt Ernie. Thus began a shared journey of learning what it means to serve others in the name of Christ. In fact, the journey transformed their lives. Hearing their story, I was moved to join them.

On bended knee, I learned that the young people and their parents had helped Ernie by listening to his needs and hopes, then surrounding him with the kind of help Ernie felt he needed. In return, Ernie pledged to live responsibly, abstaining from alcohol and drugs, showing up for appointments, and being truthful and honest in all matters. Ernie needed a doctor, so they found one who would see him free of charge, as a gift of mercy. Ernie needed a job, so one of the parents helped him prepare a resume, apply for a job, practice for his job interview, and then accompany him to the interview. When Ernie got the job, he needed a car but didn't want a handout, so they found a family who had a car they were willing to sell and wait until Ernie received his first paycheck before paying for the car. The same was true of a house. It was important to Ernie to own a home he had worked for himself. The youth and their parents, along with other church members who had joined them by this time, made it possible for Ernie to receive a loan so he would have the money to buy his dream home—a small mobile home in a stable, safe, and secure community. It was at that mobile home, Ernie's home, where I found myself on that Saturday.

These young people and Ernie treated each other like family. Ernie told us what he wanted planted and where. The young people went in and out of Ernie's home with the ease of those who know they are welcomed. Though they came from families of economic means and Ernie had just come out of poverty, I did not once notice the kind of alienation that so often rears its ugly head when there are social and economic differences between people—quite the contrary. Watching and listening, I realized that Ernie and these young people had, in the spirit of the historic Eucharistic prayer, become one. For generations, Christian disciples have prayed that they might become one with Christ, one with each other, and one in ministry to all the world. That prayer had been fulfilled in this wondrous community of faith between young people and a once-homeless man. The love among them was deep and authentic, as together they dreamed of ways to help others.

When I asked how it all happened, Ernie told me that the young people gave him a new life by loving him with the very love of Christ Jesus. The young people disagreed, saying it had been Ernie who showed them the love of Christ. He taught them about life and the sustaining grace of God. His profound gratitude deepened their commitment to being servant leaders in the world.

I could see that both answers were right. The generous sharing of Christ's love had transformed them all. And by the end of that day, I had been transformed as well.

Minerva G. Carcaño is the first Hispanic woman to be elected to the episcopacy of The United Methodist Church. She is bishop of the Phoenix Episcopal Area, and serves as the official spokesperson for The United Methodist Council of Bishops on the issue of immigration.

NOTES

1. This passage was influenced by Adam Hamilton, "Remembering True North" (sermon, July 14, 2002, United Methodist Church of the Resurrection, Leawood, KS).

2. John Wesley, "The Almost Christian" (sermon, July 25, 1741, St. Mary's, Oxford University).

3. Ibid.

4. Ibid.

5. An autobiographical account of retired archbishop Lawrence Ayo Ladigbolu can be found in Bishop Ayo Ladigbolu, "Let the Redeemed of the Lord Say So," January 23, 2012, http://cmpage.org/bishopayo.html.

6. Adam Hamilton, "Why Should We Pray?" (sermon, February 28, 1999, United Methodist Church of the Resurrection, Leawood, KS).

7. Richard J. Foster, *Prayer: Finding the Heart's True Home* (New York: Harper-Collins, 1992).

8. Ibid.

9. Louise Perrotta, *All You Really Need to Know About Prayer, You Can Learn from the Poor* (Atlanta: Charis Books, 1996), pp. 89–92.

10. From Albert Outler, *Disciple I Video* (Nashville: Abingdon Press, 2005), interview by Richard Wilkie.

11. Erik Weihenmayer, "Touch the Top," Jan. 3, 2012. http://touchthetop.com.

12. Many versions of the telegraph story are in circulation. This version is found at: "His Amazing Love and Grace," Dec. 21, 2011, http://www.his-amazing-love.org/encouraging-stories/5-gods-love-for-us/36-the-job-applicant.html.

13. "Spurned Bible" folk tales such as this one may have become popular after the 1897 publication of H. G. Wells' short story, "The Lost Inheritance" (reprinted in *H. G. Wells Complete Short Story Omnibus* [Orion Publishing Group, London: 2011]).

14. James W. Moore, *Top Ten List for Christians* (Nashville: Abingdon Press, 1999).

15. Robert Fulghum, *It Was on Fire When I Lay It Down* (New York: Random House, 1992), p. 170.

16. "Mission America 2007," January 23, 2011, http://theamericanchurch.org.

17. John Reynolds, *Anecdotes of the Rev. John Wesley* (Leeds: H. Cullingworth, Bridge-End, 1828).

18. John Wesley, "The Use of Money," *The Works of John Wesley,* vol. 6., *Sermons on Several Occasions* (Grand Rapids: Zondervan, 1958) pp. 124–35.

19. Julia Cameron and Mark Bryan, *Money Drunk/Money Sober: 90 Days to Financial Freedom* (New York: Ballantine Wellsprings, 1999), p. 13.

20. Herb Miller, "Herb Miller's Nuggets, vol. 31: Money Isn't/Is Everything: What Jesus said about the Power of Spiritual Money," December 21, 2011, www.godslove.org/resources/pdfs/herb_miller.pdf.

21. James Moore, *At the End of the Day: How Will You Be Remembered?* (Nashville: Dimensions for Living, 2002), pp. 156–57.

If you liked this book,
you'll love the church program.

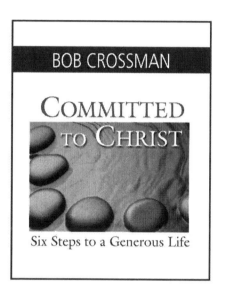

This six-week stewardship campaign includes a kickoff Sunday and six weeks of sermons, worship, study, and devotions around the six commitments of Christian discipleship: prayer, Bible reading, worship, service, financial giving, and witness.

Get more information at:
AbingdonPress.com

About the Author

Bob Crossman has over 35 years of experience as a pastor and has served as pastor or staff member in congregations from 13 to 3000 members. As Director of the New Church Leadership Institute for the Arkansas Conference of the United Methodist Church and a Ministry Strategist with Horizons Stewardship, he conducts workshops across the country on topics of holistic stewardship, developing a vision, and overcoming growth barriers in a range of settings, from new church starts to established congregations. Bob has been the recipient of the Denman Evangelism Award and received a doctorate from SMU in evangelism.